Walking

By Lori Tupper

DEDICATION

To my husband, Michael. He offered to take my chemotherapy for me and even though they wouldn't let him, I love him for the offer.

To my Children, Scott, Sarah, and Ali who created the "encouragement line" out of a clothesline, clothespins and homemade banners that kept me going through an entire year of treatment. You guys are my heart & Soul. I love you both so much!

To my nurse navigator, Jennifer; To my awesome radiation team; and to everyone who works and volunteers at the West Michigan Cancer Center— all angels in people disguise!

CONTENTS

INTRODUCTION

It is always somewhat of a shock when one is diagnosed with a medical condition that causes one to sit down to a staring contest with mortality. When that call comes in, one of the biggest decisions is to determine how you are going face your mortality on a daily basis. Are you going to be the strong silent type, bearing the entire burden alone and in secret? Are you going to only tell family members, allowing only those related to you the privilege of traveling along on the journey? Or, are you going to put it out there in the Universe and share your journey with as many people as possible? It really is a very personal decision and one that I feel can determine how your journey travels.

When I was diagnosed with breast cancer in February, 2017, I was almost "offended" that such a diagnosis would be made. I had followed recommended protocols since age 40—yearly mammograms and monthly breast exams. But suddenly a new journey was presented and my history was once again rewritten.

I am very thankful for all of my friends who read my essays throughout my journey and supported me with positive energy and prayers.

If this is a journey you are facing, I hope my writings will offer some practical ideas, knowledge, and mostly hope.

Be well!

Lori Tupper
lrtupper@gmail.com

TRIBAL COUNCIL

Wednesday, February 8, 2017

In six hours I will be having a needle biopsy on my right breast. It is 2 am and I can't sleep. I feel as though I am going to a "tribal council" tomorrow and I may be the one voted off the island.

I'm not afraid to die...just afraid of what the doctors will do to me before I make the journey.

Lord, help me.

Friday, February 10, 2017

So I had the biopsy yesterday and although there was not much pain, it was brutal.

Dr.: Okay, your name is Lori Tupper and you were born on 7-10-59 and we are doing a biopsy of your right breast and lymph node. Are you okay with that?

Me: Well, I'm not OK with it exactly. I mean, I don't WANT to be here doing this, but I understand what you are saying.

Dr: I need to hear you say you are okay with this. I take this very seriously.

What I wanted to say: Oh, and you think I'm not taking it seriously? You think I WANT to be laying on this gurney and you think I am supposed to say I am OK with you sticking a needle in my boob and clipping out pieces of tissue. In order for you to do your job, I have to say I'm okay with it? really?

What I Said: I understand what you are going to do, but I don't really feel like I have a choice.

Dr.: You ALWAYS have a choice!

What I wanted to say: Okay then. I choose to get up and walk out. I choose to not have breast cancer. I choose to erase the fear of this last week and be who I thought I was a week ago!

What I Said: This is what has been recommended. I understand what you are going to do and I give you permission to do it.

Dr: Well then, let's get started.

I wasn't intending to be uncooperative, words are just very important to me and I did not want to say I was "ok" with it. It is ok NOT to be ok with what is happening in your life.

But, I lived through the biopsy, talking about my kids and holding on to what I know to be true....trying to release the fear and terror I felt inside.

We all talked—the four of us, as the doctor worked. The girl operating the ultrasound, the nurse assisting, me, and the doctor. After the procedure was over (and really, the pain WAS minimal) I was quite proud of how brave I had been and I was just resting. The girl operating the ultrasound and the doctor left the room to look at the pictures while the nurse stayed with me and was rubbing my shoulder a bit.

Nurse: How are you doing?

Me: Oh, I am fine. It wasn't as bad as I thought it would be.
Then I became very quiet as I realized that was all probably the easy part.

Nurse: A little overwhelming, isn't it?

All of the sudden, the tears started flowing. A little bit of compassion from the nurse and I lost it!

Me: Yes. It is very overwhelming! She found me a tissue. After a few minutes of crying softly, I pulled myself together and blew my nose. The Dr. re-enters.

Dr: Okay, we are going to send you for some more pictures so we can track those markers and then I want to talk to you and your husband before you leave.

Me: okay.

The following mammogram was not as painful as it had been the week before because my breast was still numb. Afterwards, the nurse and I were talking about dogs as she bandaged me up.

Nurse: My dachshund is so tiny, but he has a big personality and loves to eat. They keep telling me he is overweight.

Me: How much does he weigh?

Nurse: I think he is around 20 lbs.

Me: See, you should have a lab. They can weigh 80 lbs. and the vet doesn't complain too much. Does she stay home when you come to work?

Nurse: Yes, she and the two cats hang out and all three are there ready to greet me when the garage door goes up.

Me: Are you married?

Nurse: I'm a widow. My husband was killed in a car accident on I-94 ten years ago.

I know she is only 40 because we already had that discussion.

Me: That's awful. I'm so sorry.

Nurse: Yes, it was pretty bad. He was with his dad. We lost them both.

Suddenly, I don't feel like the unluckiest person in the world and my self-pity vanishes for an instant.

Me: Wow. That would be awful to go through.

Nurse: It was pretty hard. I had just been diagnosed with MS

Me: You have MS?

Nurse: Yes. But the medicine seems to be working well and I'm doing pretty good.

Me: Wow.

Then it was time to talk to the Dr.
Michael is sitting next to me and all I want is to go home.

Dr: Okay. As you know, we took a biopsy of the right breast and the right lymph node. We should have the pathology report back in 2-4 days so you will either get a phone call on Friday or Monday, but I wanted to talk to you about what you are probably looking at. The tissue I extracted looks *VERY* suspicious and is most likely cancerous. I would be extremely surprised if the result is otherwise. So Jennifer here is going to assist you in other appointments you will need to schedule after you receive the phone call. She will schedule you for a surgery consult and for any other appointments you may have. She is a nurse navigator and will be your contact person in our office.

The Dr. eventually left and Jennifer gave us a "breast cancer handbook" and was very friendly.

So, I walked out with my "breast cancer handbook" thankful I did not have MS and that my sweet husband was beside me holding my hand.

And now...two days later...I will spend the day doing whatever I like, waiting for the call with the pathology results and I am okay with that.

Friday, February 10, 2017 (10:39 am)

My phone rang. It was Jennifer, the nurse navigator. Yes, she confirmed the diagnosis of malignant Invasive ductal carcinoma in both the right breast tissue as well as in the right lymph node. And so it begins...the long journey of me realizing I am mortal.

The first decision I felt I had to make was how am I going to deal with this...who am I going to tell? My instinct is to keep it all to myself, but eventually, I realize it is not fair to keep this information from my family. I tell mom and dad first. Cancer is not a stranger to our family. My father had melanoma in 1979 and amazingly is still with us. My mother has been living with leukemia for almost 15 years, and my brother-in-law died of cancer less than two years ago—but there is no history of breast cancer.

After telling my parents, I tell my kids. In my fantasy mind —I see myself flying out to where they live and telling them face to face, but it was so much easier to tell them in a sucky email— which is what I did. Michael had called each of them after our initial talk with the doctor to give them a head's up, so I knew the email would not be a total shock.

My mind keeps going back to Jane. Jane was a young lady at one of our churches who had been diagnosed with breast cancer and I remember her saying, "I started out asking God 'Why me?' and then one day it hit me, —'Why NOT me?' and I realized God is always in control." With 1 in 8 women having breast cancer—I can say the same thing and there is no reason I deserve to be exempt from suffering.

After telling my family, I told my BFF, Ruth, who could initially say nothing but, "Shit" which I found strangely comforting. With the second phone call, she graduated to, "That just sucks," which I also found very comforting.

In the midst of all this so far, I find I am exhausted—not from the cancer, I'm sure, but from the emotional processing of having cancer. I have talked to many people who have offered encouragement and support and that means a lot to me. But, I feel so very positive that no matter what happens —I win. I either get to stay with my family, or see my Jezzie—my angel in dog disguise. Either way, I am on a journey that is going to teach me so much about life and myself.

So, yes Doctor. My name is Lori Tupper, I was born on July 10, 1959. I have breast cancer and I AM okay with that.
2-13-17

PERVADING SADNESS

The sadness is ever-present. I go to bed thinking about how strong I have been throughout the day and feeling positive, but then I wake up and I still have cancer. There is no reward for being strong. I don't get a card punched for additional hours or days to live. Sometimes I want to just lay in my bed and cover my head. Sometimes I don't want encouragement or strength...I just want to disappear.

The wonderful thing about writing about the fear is that I don't have to talk to people about the fear, but find that it affects me every second of every minute, every minute of every hour and every hour of every day.

I get up in the morning and spend 15 minutes meticulously making our bed. The flat sheet edge must lay at the head of the bed until I get the blanket on the bed straight and Michael's electric blanket centered above where he sleeps. The three covers are folded down ONLY after I have centered the quilt evenly on the bed, with the bottoms of the design hanging about 2 inches over the bed mattress.

Once everything is lined up, THEN all covers are folded back until the quilt lines up with one of the horizontal designs. The two main pillows are placed on each side of the headboard with the extra white pillow placed vertically between them. Finally, the two pillows covered with green pillow shams are meticulously thrown haphazardly at an angle between the white pillows and the vertical pillow, overlapping in a V-shape at the headboard.

If Michael feels inspired to toss all the covers up over the pillows in an effort to be "helpful" by making the bed, I take everything off and start all over. Only when the bed is perfect can I begin my day of being strong again.

I don't understand this behavior as I did not used to be that way, but all of the sudden, I assume because of the state of my health, I feel the need to control SOMETHING! ...and if that something is how my bed is made, so be it.

Because my right lymph node was cancerous, I am afraid that cancer is spreading through my body as I try not to focus on it. As much as I say I'm not afraid to die, I'm scared of so many other things that keep me from living my days to the fullest. But, I just heard a song on Flight #334 to St. Croix, Virgin Islands. Catchy tune and great message...

"Gotta live the now because the tomorrow is too far away." Gonna try that for the next 8 days in the Caribbean.
2-14-17

HOLY CRAP

Now, I've always pictured my entrance into heaven a little bit differently than most people. In my mind, I am greeted by my black lab, Jezebel, and as I walk up to Jesus we do a little secret dance/handshake (high five, shimmy, hip bump, skin, and fluttering fingers). Now, after my day yesterday, I think He will lean forward with His personal message from God and whisper "Holy Crap" in my ear. We will both laugh loudly, and then my eternity will begin with my dog.

As sad as I was yesterday, I had a "moment." It happened at the Miami airport. We were rushing to a gate and all of the sudden I saw a Black Lab to my right. I immediately sensed it was there for training and that for some reason, its owner was unhappy with it.

As I was gazing at the beautiful black lab, I continued to walk pulling my luggage. Suddenly, I felt the floor soften, looked down, and realized I had just stepped in a pile of fresh dog poo. It all happened so quickly and I'm not even sure how I didn't stop and check out my shoe except that I knew we were on a mission to get to the next gate...and then I forgot about it.

On the next flight from Miami to St. Croix, I sat between Michael and another young man to my right. As I sat there the thought ran through my mind, "Wow, I think he might have eaten something that is not digesting too well...whew!" He did not say a word to me and just kept to himself the entire three hours, ignoring Michael and me.

We arrived at our destination, with great relief picked up our luggage, talked with our hosts for at least 20 minutes and then it was time to go to bed, finally. After I put on my pajamas, I noticed my one shoe had leaves and grass sticking out of the side of it. I picked it up, suddenly remembering the black lab. I smelled my shoe...Dog crap! I spent the next 30 minutes cleaning every groove of my beloved shoe to restore balance to my New Balance.

It was in the middle of the night that I woke up laughing at the irony of the situation and the analogy to my life. While in the midst of experiencing the happiest moment of my day (looking at the Black lab), I stepped in a pile of dog crap. While in the midst of experiencing some of the happiest moments of my life (retirement and traveling with Michael), I am experiencing some cancer crap.

BUT...I took the time to clean up my shoe to restore balance to my New Balance walking and that is what I will do with my health. It may take some time, but it will be okay. It may not always be a pleasant experience and it may cause me to be uncomfortable, but it will be what it is and when Jesus whispers "Holy Crap" in my ear as I enter heaven, we will both laugh loudly as eternity begins.

...I just wonder what stories that young man sitting on the plane next to me is telling about us today?
2-15-17

GOD'S INSTRUCTIONS

We were on the flight from Miami to St. Croix when I suddenly felt the air change, my heart started to race, and slight pain in my chest appeared. I took a deep breath and tried to wriggle more room into my middle seat. I have only had one anxiety attack in my life and that was on the four-story ferris wheel located in Chicago at Navy Pier. I realized now exactly what I realized then..."there ain't no quick way off this thing I'm on."

I sat back in my seat. Breathe in to the count of 4. Hold to the count of 7. Breathe out to the count of 8. Repeat. Focus. Pray. "God, just help me get to St. Croix. Once I'm there, it is okay for me to die." Breathe, Focus, Pray, Instruct God...Breathe, Focus, Pray, Instruct God. I felt answers were coming when the pilot announced we were landing 15 minutes early. Thank you, Lord.

My mind went back to 15 hours earlier when Michael and I were driving to O'Hare airport at the start of our journey.

Me: Do you believe in heaven?
Michael: Yes.
Me: What do you think it is like?
Michael: I think it is wonderful.
Me: Well, it makes more sense to me if God recycles our souls and we come back to live a different life. I mean, how can He possibly keep track of everyone if He continues to create new souls all the time? That would be a logistical nightmare!
Michael: He's God. He doesn't have to be logical.
Me: Do you think He heals people?

Michael: I think in most cases, God allows nature to run it's course, but there are a some instances where God performs miracles.

Me: What if (God close your ears, please), the only God there really is is inside of us? What if WE really control our destiny, health, and outcomes.

Michael: I don't believe in that. I believe there is a God. Me: I do too, I'm just wondering.

Ever since my diagnosis on Feb. 10, it has been like a tune stuck in my head and that is all I can think about. Along with that tune come question after question that my soulmate patiently addresses and assures me of God's presence.

We finally landed in St. Croix. The first couple of days, the cancer tune continued to play in my head constantly. I would dream about procedures and prognoses. Every song I heard at the restaurants we ate at were pointed at me. Sitting at Cheeseburgers in Paradise, I listened to the Caribbean singer crooning Bob Marley's, "Don't Worry about a thing, Everything's Gonna Be Alright" and I wondered how he knew exactly what I was going through and was sure he was singing that only for me. I actually teared up at his compassion for me. Every experience I had, I thought of as "this will probably be my last time doing this." It was becoming a strange journey.

But then, I admitted to myself..."it doesn't matter how much support others offer you or how many pricey distractions you can afford, this is a journey you have to walk alone because nobody can get you away from yourself. You are always there thinking about it and nobody can control that except you."

So, I decided to try another approach. I read through the supportive Facebook Comments and decided to go with the thread theme..."Relax, enjoy, get some rest physically and mentally."

I focused on quiet and rest. I started reading a book. I pretended like life was perfect because actually, at this point—my life HAS been perfect. I noticed I was sleeping in longer, enjoying my picture-taking again, feeling calmer. By the fourth day on the island, I realized I had actually gone a couple of hours without thinking about having cancer. By the time we came home yesterday, I was able to relax on the plane and actually, I don't think I have given God any instructions for a couple of hours now!

2-23-17

THE PRAYER

A small star flies in from left of screen and stops. It twinkles as Clarence speaks:

CLARENCE'S VOICE
You sent for me, sir?
CREATOR'S VOICE
Yes, Clarence. A man down on earth needs our help.
CLARENCE'S VOICE
Splendid! Is he sick?
CREATOR'S VOICE
No, worse. He's discouraged.

I never understood this scene from "It's A Wonderful Life," until this morning.

At 4 am, I woke up and was reviewing in my mind if I had everything packed for New Orleans since we were leaving immediately following my second biopsy if they were able to do it successfully in the office today.

As I lay there, I mentally went over the clothes that I packed when I suddenly realized I had forgotten to empty the drawers in Frakes where we stayed Sunday and Monday night. We left so suddenly on Tuesday morning when I realized they had scheduled me for a biopsy on my left breast on the first of March.

Michael packed most of my stuff but neither one of us emptied the drawers which held all my warm weather crop pants and my favored "man jams" that I like to wear if I'm really cold.

"Oh no," I said aloud.
"What's wrong?" asked Michael
"I forgot to get the clothes out of the drawers in Frakes, KY. What am I going to wear in New Orleans?"
"Don't worry about it."

I got out of bed and stood up to go to the bathroom when all of the sudden I burst into tears. No, not tears exactly—I started wailing like a child in the middle of a Walmart aisle who desperately wanted something to which her mother said "no."

"I can't do this. I can't travel, I can't deal with cancer! I just can't!"

"Come lay down. Let me hold you." Michael said. I continued to wail. I went to the bathroom and wailed the whole time. I went to the living
room hiccuping as I wailed.

I don't think I even have to explain this, but the wailing probably had NOTHING to do with the clothes I left in Kentucky. I sat in my chair and was only crying now. Michael decided to get up and have a bowl of cereal. I cried a while longer and finally was able to calm down long enough to ask Michael what was on my mind. "Why does God give you so many people to love if He's going to just take you away from them," I cried.

"I don't know" is all He said.

He gave me the yogurt I was supposed to eat for breakfast and I ate it slowly, so so scared about the day to come. I had written a note to
a friend, saying: "I don't even know what to wish or pray for since I can't control it and whatever happens is what is supposed to happen."
Her response was loving and accepting, "and when you cannot pray, that is when we all are lifting you up and supporting you with our
prayers."

I felt loved. So as I went to my appointment and lay on the table for over 2 hours while they figured the plan for a biopsy on my left breast, I felt anxious. They were going to go for it, so that meant I would probably get to go to New Orleans. They left me in the room while they organized the team. I lay there trying to find some peace.

*"The sea of life is raging, the storm clouds
around me roll
I'm tossed about in turmoil, it's growing very
cold.
By myself I'd never make it, but this one thing
I know...
when I say the name of Jesus, the storm clouds
have to go.
When I say Master, my sorrows disappear,
When I say Father, He wipes away my tears,
When I say Savior, My blinded eyes can see,
When I say Jesus, He speaks peace to me"*

It is a song I have sung for 36 years when I am alone, driving in the car, taking a shower, or working around the house. When I don't know what to sing, this is the song I sing and I've never really understood why I loved it so much as I have not had much "raging" in my life, but today as I lay on the gurney alone, waiting for the team to return, I quietly sung that song. Afterwards, I felt a peace beyond description and I thought to myself, "I guess that really IS a prayer."

So the biopsy was done. The Dr. said the samples did not look as "suspicious" as the ones on the right side had—which is good. And then we left for New Orleans.

As we were driving around Louisville, KY. I shared this experience with Michael and as I looked up, I saw a LOT and I means hundreds of "God rays." and my heart opened to hope, tossing out the fears that had gripped me only this morning and I felt God's message loud and clear...

I heard that prayer, Lori Tupper, and I am with you.

3-1-17

FROM ETHIOPIA WITH LOVE

One of the most interesting perspectives I have gained in the last year of travel, is that the world seems much smaller. People are the same everywhere you go. You see the same emotions and desires no matter what latitude or longitude you visit. People everywhere desire success, acceptance, affirmation of life, and love.

Living with cancer has given me new perspectives on every aspect of my life...how I spend my money, how I interact with strangers, how much less I care about how I look (which I never thought possible!)

While shopping with my sister-in-law in a mall in New Orleans, I passed by one of those kiosks in the center where a person tries to lure you in with a free sample that is going to make you look 10 years younger. The young black man smiled at me and I smiled back. As he beckoned me to have a seat, I found myself moving toward him knowing I could at least listen to his spiel and perhaps show some kindness.

"What is your name?" he asked.
"Lori." I said.
"Well, Lodi, I am going to show you a product that can perform miracles on your skin. Is that okay?"

"Sure," I said, remembering how old I had looked in the mirror that very morning and thinking that maybe I should care.

He had me hold out my right arm face up as he applied an astringent to it.

"My goodness, Lodi, did you take a shower this morning?" he teased as pieces of dead skin appeared on his towelette.

"I did." I said, smiling at him. "Where are you from?"

"If you can guess, I will give you this item free," he promised, holding up Step 4 in a 5 step-process. I saw through that immediately, knowing I would have to buy steps 1-3 in order to use it.

"Is it an island?" I asked. He answered no.

"Why do you think I am finding so much dead skin on your arm, Lodi?" he asked, trying to redirect my focus back to his product.

"I KNOW why." I answered, "because I put lotion on this morning and because I left my sand/coconut oil exfoliator at home.

He finished cleaning my arm and then asked me to compare it to the left arm. I noticed no difference at all, except the right was red from the astringent he had applied.

"Now, Lodi, This next step will amaze you."

Suddenly, my sister-in-law stepped up and although I did not feel rushed by her, I felt badly I was taking this young man's time when I knew I was not going to buy his product.

"Listen," I said, deciding it would be more kind to vacate the chair for maybe a real potential customer. He looked deeply into my eyes as I gave him back the sample he had given me, "I'm going to give this back to you. I don't know how long I have to live and I'm not going to spend money on something like this if I'm not sure how long I'm going to live." His jaw dropped.

We walked away and I mumbled to my sister-in-law, "What good is it to have cancer if you can't use it to get out of uncomfortable situations you get yourself into?" She laughed, "I don't think he knew quite what to say."

As we shopped in the next store, my mind went back to the young man and I realized my original intention was to show kindness to him (which I wasn't sure I had), plus, he never told me where he was from.

As we passed him again, he smiled at me and I approached him. "Hey,"I said, "you never told me where you are from"

"I am from Ethiopia," he answered.

"Well, good luck with your work. I want to explain, I was just diagnosed with breast cancer and I really don't know how long I will live." I said, wondering to myself why I was sharing this information with him. He took my hand, looking deeply into my eyes and said these words to my heart...

"Lodi, I am sorry. Just live each day to the best, and I thank you that we met."

I walked away feeling the world becoming a bit smaller because God had sent me just a little bit of acceptance, affirmation of life, and love from Ethiopia.

3-3-17

THE APPOINTMENT

After five days, I finally feel ready to share about the appointment with the surgeon where my plan was developed. It is interesting to me to watch myself and how long it takes me to "process" what is happening to me when just 2 months ago, nothing was happening at all.

We asked our friend, Linda, to join us at my visit with Dr. K. on March 10th. Linda is not only a good friend, but also a retired nurse and we felt as though three sets of ears and the emotional support would be beneficial.

"We'll go to breakfast afterwards," I naively told her. "I have to check in at 8 am, but the consultation won't be until 9. She agreed to all the specifics and I was excited to finally have a presented plan so I could get on with my life.

I checked in, presented my paperwork, was examined, and now sat in Dr. K's office with Linda between Michael and me.

Dr. K. started with the history of breast cancer treatment in a very direct, easy-to-understand way. It was helpful to see that it is an area that continues to make progress in it's diagnostics as well as in its treatments.

"Now, for you, Lori, since your lymph nodes are involved and the breast MRI has defined your tumor to be 9cm, I am recommending a modified radical mastectomy of your right breast with the removal of levels one and two of your lymph nodes, as well as a lumpectomy of the mass in your left breast immediately following."

Of course, for me—an introvert, having to sit and listen to a doctor talk about me for 45 min. is not exactly enjoyable. I tried to maintain eye contact, but spent most of my time noticing the books on her shelves, the supplies on her desk, and her haircut. She would say something every now and then that would bring me back.

"I will arrange for you to meet with the plastic surgeon to discuss reconstructive surgery which will be performed immediately following the mastectomy."

"Ummm...I don't think I'm interested in that." I said.

"Why?" she asked. Michael and I had discussed it prior to this visit and I felt firmly that I did not want something placed inside of me that was not naturally part of me for aesthetic reasons.

"Well," I hesitated, "I just don't feel like my breasts are my identity and it is not important to me. Is it important to you, Michael?"

"No." He answered.

"Ok." she said, "but you know insurance is required to pay for it for breast cancer patients." I think she wanted to make sure I wasn't refusing because of the cost.

"That's nice," I said, "but I'm not interested." Then the topic was dropped. Besides, I thought, with a prosthesis—you can choose whether or not to wear it and maybe toss it around for fun, too. But I did not speak this thought aloud.

Once again, I leave and get back to admiring her hair, wondering how long she has to spend on it in the morning. It is really cute.

"So, I'm looking at my calendar. How does April 11th sound for your surgery?" Her question pulls me back and I feel a twinge of panic.

"If she had it on the 11th, would she be able to travel overseas on the 14th?" Michael asked.

Dr. K. looked at him, "Absolutely not."

I started to cry. Not so much because that meant I could not go to New Zealand, but more because I knew the conversation was going to require

29

me to engage and interact. Also, I could not stand the thought of my entire family losing out on something we had been planning for so long because of me.

"Well, why don't we just schedule your surgery for after the trip?" Dr. K. suggested.

My tears instantly dried up. I felt like I must look like a two-year-old who thinks she can manipulate the world by having a tantrum. "Will it make a difference in the cancer?" I ask.

"No. Breast cancer is generally very slow-growing...enjoy the trip with your family and then we will take care of you."

"So, if I cry some more, will it ALL go away?" I asked, kind of laughing at how I had managed to squeeze in another trip.

"No, I'm sorry." She answered softly. And I really felt like she *was* sorry and that she really wished I could make it all disappear just by sacrificing some tears.

After meeting with Dr. K, we met with her assistant who efficiently set up appointments for surgery, a CT scan, bone scan, blood test, and an EKG. The scans would check to see if the cancer has spread to any other organs, which would totally change the treatment plan if it has.

After meeting with the very efficient Courtney, we met with the nurse navigator, Robin, who graced me with training on how to empty and measure the two drainage bags I will be released with and then assembled a Breast Cancer "goody bag" for me (sour candies to suck on during chemo, a journal, a heart pillow for after surgery, an apron to hold my drainage bags, lip balm for after surgery, and a lint brush for my head when I lose my hair after chemo). All items were placed in a pretty pink reusable bag and handed to me at the end of the meeting.

Next came the blood test and EKG. Michael, carrying the pink bag because I refused to, and Linda accompanied me to the lab and visited while I left to meet more people who wanted to talk about me.

We left the center around noon. I was starving and exhausted. The three of us went out for lunch, where I ordered a big breakfast to nourish my body with the depleted soul.
3-14-17

THE ROSARY

I'm starting to think that God might be amused with how I am dealing with all that is going on with me.

While in Italy last fall, Michael and my awesome cousin, Kris, visited a lot of the beautiful churches throughout Italy. I, feeling less enamored with the church since Michael's retirement, passed on most of these experiences. After returning from Italy, Kris sent Michael Rosary beads as a thank you for some of the planning he did. Coincidentally, my neighbor and huge supporter, Jean, mentioned praying the Rosary for her family and visited with me earlier in the week and we went over how it was done. I took Michael's rosary beads and reviewed the prayers with Jean and then felt compelled the next day to pray the rosary as I started my day.

So, today as I packed a bag for my morning at the hospital, I slipped in the rosary beads. As I sat in the waiting room after drinking an interesting contrast cocktail, I watched the sun rise over the lake next to the hospital and prayed the rosary— especially focusing on the "Our Father," and the phrase, "Thy Will be done." After praying, my mind went back to a conversation with Michael in the car first thing this morning

Me: So, why do you think you have to say so many "Hail Marys" when you pray the whole necklace? Is it to convince her to help you or is it to annoy her?

Michael: I feel it is to help your heart to focus on the actual prayer. Sometimes we don't know the words to pray and the rosary provides the words that give comfort and provide you with what you want to request.

Me: Oh, kind of like when a minister might lead someone to pray the sinner's prayer if they don't know the words to say in order to ask for forgiveness?

Michael: Right. Protestants (at least the ones we are we are familiar with) tend to encourage people to say what they feel, but sometimes you just don't know how to pray.

Me: I totally get that. I told Sheila the other day I don't even know what to pray for anymore. I think it is also kind of like the pentecostal people who allow the Holy Spirit to pray for them when they speak in tongues.

Michael: Right.

So here I was sitting at the hospital, quietly praying the rosary. It was calming for me.

Finally, the IV, then the CT scan and then the visit to the nuclear medicine room so they could shoot me full of radioactive poison (?). I felt like I was in a MacGyver episode when they extracted the hypodermic enclosed in a container 5x its size.

"You won't feel this," said the technician, "but it is a radioactive solution that will adhere to your bones between now and the time we do your bone scan this afternoon. We will see you back here at 1:30 for that."
"Okay. Thank you." I said and that was it.

After coming home, I fixed Michael and I omelettes w/ mushrooms and onions and then we had a long discussion (at my request) about possible outcomes, funeral preferences, and the upcoming weekend with our kids. Then it was time to refocus.

Me: Come into the bathroom with me.
    Michael: Why?
    Me: Just do it.
    We went into the bathroom, I turned off the lights.
Michael: What are you doing?
Me: Look at me— I'm full of radioactive serum, do I glow in the dark?

Thy Will Be done.
3-15-1

DEPRESSED, I GUESS

I am totally depressed today. What determines if you are depressed one day and not the next?

Still waiting for the Dr. to call regarding the CT scan. The fact that I got the word on the bone scan so quickly and that it was good news makes me afraid that this will be bad news since it is taking so long.

Talking to friends who are going through the same diagnosis, but sharing their good news with me is depressing. I feel like I am the only one going through it like I am going through it. Why wasn't mine caught at Stage I? I've always been faithful to my mammograms and usually did my monthly breast exam. Also, made the mistake of talking with a longtime friend whose mom died of breast cancer and dad also died of cancer...so depressing to listen to her describe the indignity of their treatments.

I just don't want to spend the remainder of my life going for stupid tests and having my only purpose be to keep myself alive for one more day.

What am I going to say to my kids tomorrow? I don't want to spend two days with them if I'm only going to depress everyone. I love them so much. THEY are the only reason I even care to go on living. Them and Michael.

Why does God give you such great people to love only to have you taken away from them? And why is it some days, I wake up and I feel so alive and positive and other days, I wake up and can't conjure up a positive thought no matter how hard I try?

...just depressed, I guess.

3-17-17

ABANDONMENT

How exactly do you set aside old "baggage" in order to deal with a "new" crisis. Of this, I am not sure. Old baggage...

Relationship at 16 months dating: Michael is finishing his first year of college and is insisting on riding his bicycle home from school (150 miles away). We have had a difficult year being apart with many moments of uncertainty. I beg him to ride home with a friend. He rides his bicycle home, having a great adventure that he enjoys reliving in his mind and aloud for the remainder of his life.

Relationship at 7 years married: I am 9 months pregnant and not well physically (toxemic). Son, Scott, arrived from South Korea and is 3 months, two weeks old. The Social worker arrived for a home visit a week ago and stated the agency would probably remove Scotty from our home since I was pregnant (taboo to have two children so close together). She said we would know sometime the following week. Michael leaves immediately on a scheduled bike trip with friend, John. I wait for the call and finally ended up calling the social worker. Am relieved to hear they are not planning to take my son from me.

Relationship at 7 years, 3 months married: I am at my mom and dad's in a neighboring state with our two infants. I have been admitted to the local hospital with neurological issues (paralysis on the left side). My mother begs Michael to come immediately, he waits 4 days because he has pressing church work.

Relationship at 30 years of marriage: I am in the hospital in Kentucky for an infectious dog bite. Michael says a prayer for me and then leaves for a scheduled canoe trip with daughter, Sarah.

Relationship at various stages: We attend family reunions of the Tuppers. Richard continuously is disrespectful of me and antagonizes me, especially ridiculing me about my weight. Michael is unable to ever stand up for me or go to bat for me. Eventually (after 30 years of marriage), I stand up for myself.

Relationship at 36 years: Our dog, Jezabel, has to be put down. Michael is unable to support me with his presence during this process. I have to do it alone, thankfully with the supportive presence of a neighbor.

Relationship at 38 years, 1 month: I am admitted to the local hospital because of chest pains. Michael leaves for a trip to Minnesota to attend his nephews graduation.

Relationship at 38 years 11 months: I will be admitted to a local hospital for a lumpectomy on my left breast and a radical mastectomy on my right breast. Michael will leave a week later for a scheduled week-long trip with his sister.

So, my kids come home for the weekend and both speak to me about Michael leaving so soon after my major surgery. They try to advocate for me and when I see it is going nowhere, I try to advocate for myself. Not surprised when it is touted as "drama" but am surprised he doesn't love me enough to make this decision without encouragement from others. Realizing that so much of the affection and attention I have received in the last 12 years was more for "the perception of others" than because he really loves me.

After dropping the kids off at the airport, I endured the hour-long "punishment" for advocating for myself…no hand holding…no pats on the leg…no heartfelt conversation. A brief apology from him for "something he apparently did wrong."

I sigh as I realize…abandonment is real. I guess I should not be surprised as I carry the past baggage around in my soul.

3-20-17

THE RIDGES OF HELL

"Think positive," "See the glass half full, not half empty," "Find the positive," "Look on the bright side," "Be strong," "Don't let the devil get you down," "You are strong," "You got this," these are all things crazy people have said to me.

I hiked the ridges of hell last week. I crawled past blackened caves of possibilities and peered in. And in my world where I often forget where my keys are and who is married to Faith Hill, I have to document these lessons I am learning lest I forget.

When I had my CT/bone scan last Thursday, I was told I would have the results within 1-2 days. The fact that the bone scan result came in on the same day skewed my thinking and presented that as day 1 for me (Yes, sometimes I even forget how to count, I guess). Of course, there is the weekend in that 2-day count, so now we are at a possible 4-day wait. That, in itself is not a bad thing necessarily. I have waited four days for many things…a dentist appointment to have a tooth fixed, a doctor's order to be discharged from a hospital, an answer from a friend as to whether she is going to accompany me to an event, etc. so even four days is not an unreasonable wait, but this time was different. The goal was to find out if cancer had spread throughout my bones and body. If it had, I would begin chemo immediately and the New Zealand trip would be off. If it had not, I would go to New Zealand and enjoy that trip with my family.

I thought about this journey and made a poor choice on Thursday after I had completed my tests. I thought, "If I expect the worst, then I will be prepared for it and I will be happy when I don't hear the worst." Makes sense, right?

The bone scan result came back within hours. It was clear and only showed the extensive arthritis I already knew I had—nothing cancer-related. I was euphoric! But then I packed a backpack full of the heavy rocks of hopelessness, doubt, anxiety, worry, anger, fear, and sadness. Then did I begin my hike on the ridges of hell.

Michael was gone all day on Friday, so I had plenty of time to indulge in what I saw in those blackened caves of possibilities. I waited anxiously for the doctor to call and refused to answer the phone if it was anyone identified other than the doctor. By the time Michael came home seven hours later, I was a wreck. I asked him to call our nurse navigator to see if the doctor would possibly call on Saturday or Sunday because I knew I could not spend the weekend in this same state of mind. He called. She said, no. If I didn't hear by five o'clock on Friday, I wouldn't hear until sometime on Monday.

Dinner at my friend's house was a great distraction as was a visit from the kids on Saturday and Sunday. Of course, we had hoped we would have all the information by the time they had arrived so we could make definite plans for the New Zealand trip. Instead, we had to talk in possibilities to be determined on Monday. These possibilities not only included travel, but also non-travel and at my request, funeral arrangements (just in case).

I made my desires known for the service and "committal" party. Scotty's response made me smile, "Sounds like a fun party, mom…hope it's one we don't have to have soon."

After we dropped the kids at the airport around noon on Monday, I found myself on a swift toboggan down a slippery slope. I continued thinking of all the worst possibilities and where I would die…Should I be secluded on a hospital bed in my office so no one has to be around my dying self or should I set up in the dining room where I could enjoy the sunlight and outdoor? (the sled moved faster), Will I be able to toilet myself? (…picking up speed), Will hospice need a key to the house? (…and faster), Will anyone be with me at the end? (…and now it was slowing because I was so close to the bottom).

It was only 2:30. I was exhausted and sitting in my chair crying. Michael (the other victim in this illness) sat on the couch watching me, unsure of what to do with this snotty mess I had become.

I couldn't bear it any longer. I got up and went to the bed. Laying down could not bring me any lower than I already was. I was done. I couldn't do this. I am NOT as strong as everyone says I am. Michael came in and lay next to me, holding me tightly.

"I can't do this," I cried. "I just want this over with now. I can't do this slow death thing. I just need to end this misery." I was shocked at the words that were flowing from my mouth. I had never spoken such words aloud and they scared me. "What will I do if the doctor doesn't call me tonight? I can't make it like this until morning."

Michael just held me tightly. A few minutes later, I felt energy coming out of his body.

"Let's watch TV." he said.

I looked at him incredulously, "What?"

"You need to distract your mind. Let's watch TV. You've been trying to get me to watch old episodes of 'Friends,' let's do it!"

I love the sitcom 'Friends,' because it makes me laugh, so I agreed. We turned on Netflix.

As each episode ended, I would say, "well, she still hasn't called yet." and then we would start another episode. In the middle of the fourth episode, at 4:30 pm, the phone rang. Michael quickly turned the TV off.

"Hello?" I answered.
"Hi Lori, Dr. Kalinowski here. Got the results of the CT scan back today and it was pretty much what I expected. 4-5 small nodules here and there, but not anything to worry about."

"But there ARE nodules?" I confirmed, not quite ready to hike back to a place of light.

"Yes, but as I told you, that is quite common. We see that in about 20% of our patients. In fact, they are so small, they couldn't even be biopsied, but we will follow up with another CT scan in three months. okay?"

"Okay." I said, hanging up the phone.

The problem with hiking the ridges of hell and allowing yourself to look into those dark caves of possibilities is that in order to get back to the light, you have to hike back.

I hung up the phone and repeated the information to Michael. I still felt incredibly sad.

"That's good, honey," he said.

I looked at him blankly. "It is? I have nodules."

He laughed as he rolled out of bed. "C'mon, let's go celebrate." We called my parents to give them the news and then the kids. Then we went to my best friend's house to tell her and her husband. THEN, we enjoyed a celebratory dinner in South Haven. And, with each positive thing we did and each person I shared my news with, I was able to remove one of the heavy rocks and by the time I got back home around 9:00, the ridges of hell were behind me.

But I learned a huge lesson. I took a side trip that was not necessary and that could easily have destroyed me if I had not had my hiking partner that could recognize the dangerous terrain ahead and detour me around dangerous parts of the path.

I had traveled so far down, I could not even comprehend the good when it happened. It is a hike I will avoid at all costs. THIS is why positive thinking can make a difference in health. THIS is why you look on the bright side of things and find the positives, THIS is why you stay strong. THIS is why it is imperative to focus on NOT the IMPOSSIBILITIES, but on the I'M POSSIBILITIES!! and this is why you listen to the crazy people.

3-20-17

HEROES

Ironically, in 2002, I participated in a 3-day walk for breast cancer research, sponsored by Avon. I was pulled into this adventure by my friend, Ruth, and we both trained diligently, gathered sponsors, and between the two of us raised over $4,000.00 for breast cancer research.

As part of that adventure, I sent out a monthly newsletter to my supporters that included my training notes, some history of breast cancer research, current breast cancer statistics, a memorial to someone I knew who died of breast cancer, and my tally of donations. I found those newsletters buried in the bottom of my desk today and would like to share my "post walk" article that summed up the 60-mile walk from Ann Arbor to Detroit:

"On May 31st, 3,500 walkers from around the U.S. gathered in Ann Arbor, MI to begin our 60-mile walk to Farmington Hills, MI (Detroit suburb). There were people of all sizes, shapes, colors, ages, fitness levels, mental levels and genders. All joined together for one cause—stopping breast cancer.

To begin with, the #1 lesson I learned? WE ARE ALL CONNECTED. Every life and every death affects us all. It is our responsibility to care for each other emotionally, physically, spiritually, and mentally.

The three days for me were spent getting to know as many people as I could. "Are you walking in honor of someone?" "Are you walking in memory of someone?" "Can you tell me why you are walking?" These are the questions we heard everywhere we went. and if for a minute you forgot WHY we were walking, we would pass a couple of ladies and they would be discussing what their diagnosis was and how it affected their lives. Or, they would be sharing how chemo affected them. We couldn't forget the cause.

Out of 3,500 walkers, 175 of them were men. There were also over 300 volunteer crew people. These were the people challenged to care for the walkers and to do anything in their power to make us smile. Maybe it would be wearing a Santa beard and a hula skirt at a pit stop. Whatever it took—when we thought we couldn't walk another step—a crew person was there to clap for us, calling us "heroes" just for walking.

But, let's talk about the REAL heroes.

The first night, I went into the "Remembrance tent" at camp. This was a tent where you were invited to write on the canvas walls a special message to someone who might of died of or had breast cancer. I walked in alone. While soft music played in the background, I wrote short messages to three of my friends who had died of breast cancer. As I turned to leave, I saw a young girl crying softly and writing on the other side of the tent. I glanced at the name of the loved one she was writing to. "Mother..." To me, she was a hero.

The second day, Ruth and I met two ladies—mother and daughter. When we asked if they were walking in memory of someone, the mother looked at her daughter (as only a mother can), slipped her arm around her and said, "No, I'm walking in honor of my daughter here. She is a breast cancer survivor."
To me, they were heroes.

The closing ceremony came and 3500 walkers, all dressed in blue victory shirts, marched down a football field in rows of 40, holding the hands of their neighbor and lifting it high to show unity and victory. The walkers were divided on both sides of the stage and everyone danced to the energizing music, waving their shoes. I felt the pride of having walked (only 30 of the 60), but knowing every mile had made a difference. After all the walkers were situated on both sides of a partitioned waist-high wall, the music switched to a soft, accepting tune as hundreds of survivors, dressed in pink t-shirts marched down the partitioned "chute." Each survivor was at a different stage in their journey, many of them still bald from their chemo. As they passed each group of walkers, the walker knelt to honor them. The wave of kneeling brought tears to the survivors eyes. I could see and feel their intense gratitude for life and to us for caring. At that moment I knew…I encountered many journeys when I signed up for this walk, but these people had been on a journey that was tougher than I could ever imagine and they, well, they are the real heroes.

HIDE AND SEEK

Denial is blessed. When I tell someone that I have Stage 2B breast cancer, I long for the gift of denial. I long for the hope of life and the opportunity to appreciate the re-stained deck this summer. I try to stay positive and I try to run from the sadness, but it finds me like a child playing hide-and-seek and it runs oh so fast and tags me, laughing at the disappointment in my eyes as I reluctantly give in and allow those evil thoughts of "failure to survive" to permeate my brain.

The Rosary, some music, Bible readings, and prayer can reinstate some hope, granting me some relief from the realities. But the pervading sadness and fear eats away at my soul.

The year was 2006 or 2007. We lived in Frakes, KY and I was exhausted from teaching in a class that included a severely emotionally impaired child that was verbally abusive to me on a daily basis. I had just spent my Sunday morning with the children at our small mission church and I was done. I love kids and I especially loved the kids at that church, but on this day—I was done. I had spent every emotional asset inside of me and I had nothing left.

"I'm running away today." I announced to Michael when I got home from church. "I have nothing left to give to anybody anywhere—not even you." He looked at me and knew I meant business.

"I'm running away, too," He said. "Can I come with you?"

"Only if you do the driving," I agreed. So we ran away together. We drove up to Berea, KY and spent the day walking around some shops in that college town and enjoyed an artisan center. After a late dinner out, we returned to our beautiful mountain parsonage, renewed and re-energized.

One of the most surprising things about cancer is the emotional roller coaster I find myself riding. I don't even like roller coasters!

Yesterday, I found myself falling quickly into the pit of despair and even though I didn't have a good reason for it, I found fear paralyzing me. When I get that way, I envy everyone around me because they can do what I want to do, but can't…they can get away from me. And even though I can pray, read my Bible, say the rosary, play music, watch funny movies, etc. it just feels like I am erecting my tent under an elephant that will eventually lay down to rest.

So…Michael and I ran away…again! We went on a "coin trip." We packed only our medications and a few snacks for the car. We drove to the end of the driveway. Using a penny (because we were at a T), we flipped it. Tails, we turn left, Heads we turn right. It was an exercise in giving up control and downplaying our expectations. We drove, flipping the penny every time there was a choice of two directions (left or right) and dropping 3 pennies on a flat surface if there was a choice of three directions (1 heads up—we turned right, 2 heads up—we turned left, 3 heads up—we went straight). We let the coins decide every time we were at a stop light or at a T. We started around 3:30 in the afternoon and drove over 50 miles, ending up in Sturgis, MI. At 6:00, we stopped in Battle Creek for pizza before heading home.

Somewhere along the journey, we went over a beautiful covered bridge and then stopped by a lake for some pictures. We were amazed at the beautiful Southern Michigan countryside that we had never traveled before and eventually became comfortable with letting the coins decide where we were going to go. I even got to the point where I enjoyed being with myself.

All to say, this cancer journey is not a fun one and it is the scariest one I have ever been on. Just when I think I have everything under control, the fear and sadness finds me like a child playing hide-and-see and it runs oh so fast and tags me, laughing at the disappointment in my eyes as I reluctantly give in and allow those evil thoughts of "failure to survive" to permeate my brain. I'm not a very competitive person, but damn it, this is one hide-and-seek game I'm going to win. I'm not just here for the fellowship this time!!!!

TURNING LEFT

The year was 1975. Michael and I were traveling to our soon-to-be "college" for an open-house event. We had already driven 3 hours and should be arriving within 15-20 minutes when we came to a T. He asked me to look at the map to see which way we were supposed to turn. It was our second date.

I obligingly looked at the map, which made absolutely no sense to me. Too embarrassed to tell this young man I had no clue how to read a map, I figured I had a 50% chance of getting the answer correct by guessing.

"Uh, it looks like you need to go left," I concluded.

"Thank you." he said, gracing me with a smile and a squint from his piercing brown eyes that made my heart race.

How could I admit to him that I didn't know how to read a map? When he was mapping out road trips for his family as a child, I was gazing at houses my family would pass on the road—imagining what the people inside were like and how they were interacting with each other. While he was reading every road sign aloud while traveling with his grandparents, I was in a car somewhere watching raindrops moving upwards on a windshield, racing to an imaginary end while I predicted the winner and imagined what kind of celebration party they would enjoy. While Michael would pick up a map out of pure curiosity and map a route from Indiana to Florida, I wouldn't dream of opening an atlas just for the fun of it.

So, I wasn't too surprised after a 15-mile drive in the wrong direction when he said, "Are you sure we should have turned left at the T? We should have been there by now."

"I don't know, maybe we were supposed to turn right." I confessed.

He turned into a driveway, took the map into his own hands, studying it closely.

"Yep, right." he said as he turned around.

I've always been thankful he didn't determine my worth by how much I understood maps.

I continued to struggle with directions for much of my adult life, adopting the strategy of driving until I saw something "familiar" if I got lost.

I remember one particular trip, my first one driving from Ludington, MI to South Haven. I knew the key was to go south on Hwy 31. Once I managed to get on the highway, I noticed the roadside sign said, 31 north. My first thought was, "Oh no, that sign is wrong!" It was only after seeing 3 more signs that I assumed were "wrong" that I entertained the thought that I might be going the wrong way. But, I eventually always got to where I was going.

That first year of college, Michael was going to be speaking at a church only about 50 miles from where I lived and he wanted me to come and see him. Our family station wagon was not available, but Michael's parents graciously allowed me to borrow theirs—aptly named, "The Tank."

I thought I couldn't get very lost in 50 miles, but I continued to amaze myself. I don't think it was that I was stupid, I just think I didn't have much interest in knowing where I was going. As I drove aimlessly around Frankfort, IN looking for the church, I heard a loud crunch. Now, I'm not even sure I can understand what exactly happened, I just know that when I got out of the car, there was a "No Parking" sign sticking out from underneath the back passenger door. To this day, I am unsure of HOW anyone could run over a No Parking sign, but I did. Luckily, there was just a scrape on the car and I eventually found the church.

Eventually, I did learn to read maps but technology changed shortly after I learned such that I was kind of sorry I wasted so much of my time and energy learning something that I could then just punch into a maps program.

I see this as kind of an analogy to my health issues these last three months.

I find myself thrilled that someone else is planning my journey for me and it is someone who is REALLY GOOD at reading the health maps and someone I trust.

Of course, I believe the ultimate map reader is putting all of the right people in my path to help me. I believe that is what all the prayers of my friends enlist.

Because HE knows if all the decisions were left up to me, I would have probably just laid down and given up three months ago. HE knows that my energy disappears quickly and that I tend to wander around until I find something familiar. HE knows that I would just turn left.

THE POLYFIL BOOB DEBUT

"If You Want to See God smile, tell Him Your plan!"
~Woody Allen

This is definitely one of my favorite sayings as I believe it depicts how we try desperately to live out our expectations for ourselves and others. If life did exactly according to plan, I can't even imagine how boring it would be.

In 1978, I married my best friend and soulmate. I anticipated we would wait a few years to have children, have LOTS of them, and I would then spend my days writing books in my spare time. AND THEN GOD SMILED and after 8 years of infertility, testing, and miscarriages, we adopted a beautiful baby boy from South Korea and I gave birth to a beautiful baby girl—all within a few months. As I adjusted my expectations, I happily parented the two best babies in the world for two months, I then suffered a major stroke. AND THEN GOD SMILED as through all of this, I counted on support from others as I readjusted my expectations. My writing took a back seat as I focused on a teaching career (NEVER IN MY PLAN) and life went on.

So, yesterday, I once again woke up anticipating my day. I had a plan—A trip to the hospital to have them look at my port which had become painful and then lunch with some friends. Since it was my first "public appearance"(since my mastectomy) and to add to the excitement of the outing, I decided to wear my post-surgical camisole w/ a polyfil fake boob on the right side so my outfit would "fit" a bit better and just to see if I could manage that system. Since i was still too sore to wear a bra, it was a bit of a challenge to get the right boob to "hang" like the left one, but I worked at it, pulling, tugging and shaping as I went. Finally, dressed in my simple button-up black dress wearing a brown and black striped blouse over it as a jacket, I was ready to go.

Arriving at the hospital, I discovered the seatbelt had reshaped my polyfil breast, giving it a diagonal crevice. I reshaped it as I was walking into the hospital, hoping that IF anyone was watching that it was a patient who was having a really bad day and maybe watching my little show would make them smile.

Living through the appointment at the hospital, we moved on to the restaurant for lunch with our friends. I discovered each time I hugged someone, my body took on a different form. I honestly felt someone could get as much enjoyment out of watching my different transformations as they could laying in a field watching clouds form different animal shapes.

After ordering my lunch, I sat down with my two friends and immediately felt as though I had a polyfil third chin. Looking down, I tried to pull my camisole lower, of course announcing my intention as I manipulated my right side by pressing, pushing, and pulling.

When I finally got in the car to go home, I sighed heavily as I noticed the polyfil boob close enough to my right shoulder to be used as a pillow.

I know the changes ahead will take some readjusting...mentally, emotionally, and definitely physically...I just hope I don't embarrass those around me too often with my inability to do it without great showmanship.

Overall, the debut of the polyfil boob was a success and God? Well...I'm pretty sure GOD SMILED.

THE JIGSAW PUZZLE

On almost any given day of the year, you can walk into our home and in the corner of the dining room you will see a white 8-ft. table with a 1,000-piece jigsaw puzzle on it completed to some degree. The puzzles live in our entry closet before brought to life by our evening sessions of togetherness. We choose puzzles that are appealing to us or have special meaning (like the one of Venice, Italy) and then we order them from White Mountain Puzzle Company because the pieces are larger and they specialize in nostalgic scenery as well as interlocking pieces. We approach the puzzle in different ways as we get into it, but the first step is always the same...assemble the edge pieces in order to assess where it will go on the table. We also bought special "sorter" trays so we can sort the pieces and stack the trays in order to save space. Sometimes we will go days without working on the puzzle, but more often we will spend a day or two each week, sitting side by side, working together to recreate the picture on the front of the box propped on the stand before us, sometimes referencing color and sometimes referencing shapes.

I remember my older sister, who is an expert at doing jigsaw puzzles telling me about puzzle challenges where the participants have to do the puzzle without having a picture to reference, or having pictures on both sides of the puzzle so the participant is always unsure of which picture they are really trying to complete. There are also puzzles that are all one color so you have to rely on shape processing alone and of course there are 3D puzzles which require you to actually build something dimensionally out of puzzle pieces.

I have been thinking about puzzles a lot in the last few months as I feel like on February 10th, 2017 we were told we were going to participate in a puzzle challenge when we were given my cancer diagnosis. On March 10th, 2017, we were given a picture of the puzzle when my surgeon presented her recommendations to us in the form of a mastectomy, lumpectomy, and lymph node removal. The puzzle box was handed to us on April 25th, 2017 when I woke up from my surgery, and finally all the pieces were given to us on May 24th, 2017 when we spent three hours meeting with doctors, nurses, and social workers as they presented the recommended treatment plan at the West Michigan Cancer Center. And today, we received the details of how we will start to put that puzzle together on Friday, June 16th, at 9 am with a 6-hour chemo infusion.

In some ways, our puzzle pieces are challenging, in that we know the picture of a healthy, cancer-free body is the picture propped up in front of us that we are trying to attain, but there may be some pieces that will be difficult to interlock because of 40 possible side effects that may distract us or require us to complete smaller sections before inserting them into the big picture puzzle...and because of the aggressiveness of the upcoming treatment, I have the constant nagging feeling that this puzzle may have a few more than 1,000 pieces.

But, that is okay. Although I am not known as one of those champion puzzle participants and I wouldn't dream of entering such a challenge voluntarily, I am so blessed to have someone sitting in the chair next to me, reminding me to turn on the light when the natural light is clouded by a dark day or sunset. He sorts the pieces for me, randomly rubbing my back and giving me whole sections to complete. When I am tempted to pity myself, God reminds me to stand back a bit from the overwhelming big picture, say a prayer of thanks for the many who are supporting me, and to just start putting it together...one piece at a time...one day at a time...one step at a time...one minute at a time, if necessary.

And somehow I know that when the picture is complete—it will never be quite what anyone expects. It will be more than a healthy, cancer-free body. It will be a spirit of peace and thankfulness. It will be eyes that see every leaf on every tree, hands that hug closer and hold longer, It will be less anger, more forgiveness, more swimming, less sitting, more smiles, fewer tears and way more music...loud, smooth, heart-tickling jazz...and maybe even some dancing with the guy who sits next to me at the puzzle table, reminding me to turn on the light when the natural light is clouded by a dark day or sunset working together to recreate the picture on the front of the box propped on a stand before us.

FOREVER FRIEND

We were driving south toward I-94 after spending a day in Ann Arbor, MI to head back to Southwest Michigan.

"Do you know where you are going?" Ruth asked me.
"Yep. I know exactly where I am!" I said to her in my "pre-GPS" voice. "We will run into I-94 any minute now and will head West to get back home, hopefully before dark."

"Okay," she said, sitting back in her seat, "as long as you know."

She always believes in me. She is my Forever friend and confidant. She knows EVERY secret I have and is able to keep them close to her heart. We have traveled together, have tromped around Chicago in matching fanny packs, have spent weeks together in Florida exploring and looking for trouble. The only time I have ever been drunk, she stayed up with me all night—making sure I threw up in a waste paper basket and not all over the complimentary time share we were staying in. She was queen of the wet washcloth. We painted a school room floor together, managed to teach kids nobody else thought could learn, and I even sat with her at my son's wedding. I can tell her what I feel and she listens. She doesn't always agree with me and will tell me so. We watch every Super Bowl together and her husband sold us our first John Deere tractor. We love celebrating St. Patrick's Day together and even took a trip to Chicago for the parade, which had happened the weekend BEFORE. But, that was okay—we are used to "messing up" and changing our plans. We have painted together, taken pictures together, taught together, laughed together and cried together. People think we look like sisters and so we claim that relationship.

I look up at a road sign when I hear Ruth groan. "Toledo, OH 49 miles. I don't think we are going to be home before dark." Ruth laughs.

"I thought sure this road connected up with 94 West. I guess it doesn't" I confessed.

"You know, Lori, I didn't think it did, but you are just so damn confident that you know what you are doing that I just can't argue with you."

"I know. I hate that about myself." I confess to my directionally challenged impairment. "Wanna stop and get a cappuccino or should we visit Toledo?"

"Cappuccino, please."

Right before I went into surgery on Tuesday, Michael kissed me on my lips, and told me he loved me. Scotty kissed me on my cheek and said the same. And then, my forever friend, Ruth, kissed me on the forehead and said it, too. It was awesome to feel the love of a friend as I faced one of the most difficult surgeries of my life.

Now, the irony hits me as I remember she was the one who pushed me in the year 2001 to do a 60-mile walk for breast cancer. And even though we didn't make it the entire 60 miles, between us we raised almost $5,000.00 for breast cancer research that may play a part in saving my life. On that walk, she ruptured a disk in her spine but pressed on in pain, because she didn't want to let me down. She gives me strength in her example of living and I don't want to let her down.

Thank you, my forever friend, my sister, my travel companion, queen of the wet wash cloth, believer in me. I love you, too.

CAMP SONGS AND T-SHIRTS

Thirty years ago when I had a major stroke and could not walk straight, sit through a worship service without inappropriate laughing, read with comprehension, or compute numbers; I handled it by deciding to sell all the living room furniture when Michael went to Annual Conference and then later taking saxophone lessons. When I had to go to "Happy Bladder Camp" because of recurrent UTIs, I wrote a camp song, ("On top of Ol' Smokey, all covered with snow, I lost my poor bladder when I had to go. I wet on my blue jeans, it poured on the floor. Next time I will kegal before I open the door.") When I spent 8 days in the hospital for an infected dog bite, I worried about the dog and made friends with the other patients on my floor. So, you can imagine my surprise at the random sobbing I have experienced since my breast cancer diagnosis in February.

Yesterday was especially a wet cheek day and I have discovered that when I have to go for tests related to the cancer, it is especially difficult to keep the tears in check. After an echocardiogram and a blood test yesterday—neither of which were painful, my dental appointment had me sobbing as soon as I returned to my car. Not so much because of the physical pain as much as the discomfort of trying to share my new "health status." There is a certain amount of "re-identification of who I am" and that is not comfortable for me.

After crying off and on all day, I defiantly told Michael "I don't WANT to have chemo and radiation." His response? "Let's go to Chinn Chinn's for supper (my favorite restaurant). My pity party continued when we arrived to find they are closed on Mondays, so we settled for Cracker Barrel.

Only after we left the chaos of our home (the kitchen drain had been clogged for over a week and Michael had been working with our contractor friend to solve the problem for 3 days), did Michael address my statement regarding chemo and radiation.

"Dear, remember how anxious you were about traveling overseas in Italy when neither of us had any idea how it would go?"

"Yes,"

"Well, this is kind of like that. Remember how you totally trusted me to read the right books so we would know how to use public transit and where to go and where to stay? Remember my best friend, Rick Steves—the travel guy—who I consulted all along the way?"

"Yes." I agreed, remembering how successful our year of travel had been, thanks to the writings of Rick Steves.

"Well, It is like the cancer center is Rick Steves. We have to trust them. And, just like our trip—some things won't go smoothly and some things will go like clockwork. we just don't know what it is going to be like because we have never been on this journey before. But, we have to trust the doctors because they have helped so many others who have been on similar journeys. They are our Rick Steves."

"I know you are right." I said, "but I'm tired of thinking about it. I'm tired of waiting. I just want to be done with it all."

"Yes. I understand," he said, reaching over to run his finger down my cheek. "and it is okay not to want it. AND if at any point you don't think you can handle the treatment, you can decide what you want to do and I will be behind you 100%. But think of it as one of our trips. It will be a year full of surprises, but at least we will face those surprises together."

Later when we got ready for bed, I decided to sleep in a t-shirt and pulled one out that must of shrunk since I bought it in New Orleans. It is the first time I've worn a tight-fitting t-shirt since my mastectomy. I put it on, looked in the mirror and immediately burst into laughter at the sight of my left mountainous breast next to the flat surface of the right side of my chest. I paraded myself proudly in front of Michael and I thought to myself, "I really should work on a cancer camp song!"

When you have a serious illness and the drain clogs, your dentist says you have a few surface cavities, and your favorite restaurant is closed,—it feels hopeless—like life is just out to get you. It is so lovely when someone can pull you back a bit and help you to rebuild a better perspective... with words and a t-shirt that is too tight.

5-9-17

HOMEOSTASIS

I sat at the piano in Mr Burford's piano studio waiting for him to listen to my assigned playings for the week. I had decided to take lessons from him a year earlier because I was in love with a young man who was called to the ministry and I felt like I could do my part by learning how to play the piano better. After all, that's what a minister's wife does, isn't it?

Mr. Burford and I enjoyed talking and had an easy friendship going, but on this particular day I was eager to move along. "Mr. Burford," I asked meekly, "don't you want me to play my assignments for you?"

He sat there quietly for a moment, cleared his throat, and finally replied, "Lori, I really don't think this is your gift." Simple and true. I struggled significantly and he was right. It was not my gift. I had been toying with the idea of quitting, but this confirmed that IF I was ever going to be a minister's wife, playing the piano was not going to be a part I was going to play in that role.

"Well," I responded to Mr. Burford, "I'm not going to pay you $9 a week to be my friend. I have friends so I guess I will quit." I never went back.

I think of memories like this and wonder what was going on. Did he really say that to me or was it something I put into my own thoughts? I honestly don't know. And yet, I can see where God uses such incidents later in life to bring growth and determination to the person I have become.

Having cancer for me means I have so little control over so much of my life. I'm putting drugs into my body that I don't understand a lot about. I have feelings popping out of every emotional pore. I am learning so much about myself at warp speed and moving into an ultra sensitive state of life.

When this all started, I felt like I was in a downward spiral, moving quickly out of control into an alternative universe. Ultimately, feeling the need for homeostasis and groundedness, I designed for myself a "12-step" program to bring some routine and focus to each day. I figured if I have to spend my days avoiding public places and people, I needed to at least have a routine of things I COULD do.

Giving myself permission to choose things I can still do gave me a sense of control of at least a small part of my world. My 12-step plan:
Make the bed
Get dressed
Devotions
Yoga joint rotations
Walk on the treadmill
Gratitude journal
Eat healthy
Keep a food journal
Practice the piano
Drink 12 C. water a day
Write
Do something fun

They are not hard things, but they are things I can do and they are all things that are good for me. So, I have my little checklist for each day and when I get up in the morning, I have my focus.

BUT, I also give myself permission to NOT do something on my list if I don't feel like it or if I just don't want to. But, the one thing I do love doing every day is practicing the piano.

Mr. Burford, you were a good conversationalist for sure, but you were wrong. Playing the piano IS my gift—it is my gift from the Creator given to me long ago so I could unwrap it every day to feel grounded as I crawl out of downward spirals into my beautiful world of homeostasis.

CRYING CONUNDRUM

The headache all day yesterday was pretty intense. Since I hardly ever have them, it caught me by surprise and I assumed it was the steroid I had to start the day before my chemo, or the dental work that day repairing a few fillings, or allergies, or the fact I could not have caffeine the day before, day of, or the day after chemo. OR, maybe it was just anxiety related to the anticipation of chemo. Nevertheless, once I narrowed the headache cause down to these five possible causes, I found I could not sleep because of it.

"You are going on a journey of healing through chemotherapy. You will be fine. Decide on a friend who has passed on to walk beside you on this journey," the voice on a guided meditation for those taking chemo said on the YouTube site. I chose my dog, Jezzie, to walk the journey with me and imagined her there by my side. My headache intensified while I took a break for a few minutes to shed tears for the loss of her after she had rescued me for 8 years.

"As you approach your medical facility, enter it with a smile saying aloud, 'This is the place God is going to use to heal me...You smile at each person you meet and thank them for the services they offer. They are your team, you are their captain and you are going to be fine...you feel positive energy with your medical team and you appreciate all the efforts they put forth to make you comfortable. Picture your comfort and the bags of healing they are hanging to help your body to gain control over cancer cells with chemotherapy. You will be fine..."

For 42 minutes, I listened to the guided meditation, resting deeply. As she brought me back to the moment, I found the hardest part was saying "thank you," and then "good-bye" to Jezzie as I returned to my headache and anxiety.

I thought of this meditation as I awoke this morning (after about 2.5 hours of sleep). I practiced in my mind doing and saying what was suggested to me in the meditation. I woke up, got dressed, made my bed, packed my chemo bag, and met Michael in the kitchen.

"I can't do this." I sobbed. "I'm gonna be too hot in that cubicle."
"It's okay, we will take your fan." He packed the fan in the car.
"I didn't sleep last night and I still have my headache."
"You should have awakened me."

"No, then nobody would have slept." I started sobbing. "Dear, let's not do this now, it is time to go." I felt like a two-year being dragged to a church nursery for the first time.

I sulkingly fixed an egg sandwich to eat in the car while Michael quietly packed the car with the same amount of bags we would take for a weekend at my mom and dads.

The drive to Kalamazoo was quiet, until I started sobbing halfway there and sobbed until we were about a mile away. I blew my nose on Subway napkins from the glove box as we arrived. My head was throbbing. We had arrived early, hoping it would speed up our day and just unsure of what to expect.

Lab work on the first floor was done quickly. Remembering my meditation, I smiled at the lady who registered me and the young man who drew my blood, I talked with him a bit, and thanked him profusely for a job well done.

Then to the lower level to see the Dr. who was running an hour late due to "unexpected" events. It did not bother me too much as I knew if it was me who was in need of extra time, I would want her to take it, but I wasn't sure if it was typical. Mostly, I was worried it would affect my infusion schedule. A friend of mine works there, ran my labs and had come down to give me a hug (such a nice bonus) and I was just working on patience. So far, the smiles were easy to come. Everyone I came in contact with was so kind.

After an hour of waiting and knowing I'm not the most patient person, I asked the receptionist if this was typical. I was nice, but I was intent on trying to process this "new normal." She assured me it was not typical at all, so I felt better. It also helped that the "free treats" cart came around then with some awesome cookies and decaf for dunking.

Finally seeing the doctor, we got the okay for the infusion. Labs were acceptable, echocardiogram was good, and I was already on overload with conversations about me.

Up to second floor of the infusion lab...finally! Let's get this over with. One of my major anxieties was whether or not they would be able to access my port. We checked in with Kelli, who was a young, exceptionally nice girl, probably 22 years old.

She quickly went over the process with us, "I will walk you back today since this is your first time and the nurses will take such good care of you and make you very comfortable" I thought of my meditation and looked up to smile and say thank you, but instead I burst into tears.

The poor girl. I don't think she knew quite what to do. "In fact, I will call a nurse right now and they will take you back as soon as possible, okay?" I kind of think she thought maybe I wasn't a very good poster child for the infusion waiting room. "I'm sorry." I sobbed even harder. Michael grabbed our three bags and led me to a group of chairs. We sat. I sobbed. Kelli came over and asked if I would like some water. I gave her my glass and she filled it and brought it back to me. I went to the bathroom to splash cold water on my eyes and when I got back, she was ready to lead us back to the infusion room.

The nurse, Jillian, offered me the cubicle right next to her work station (so she could keep an eye on me no doubt). I just wanted to get started and thought that was fine. I thought once I had washed my face with cold water, I was fine. But then Jillian said, 'So how are you doing?" I thought of my meditation and looked up at her to smile and once again burst into tears. The kinder she was, the more I sobbed. The more compassion she showed, the more I sobbed. I sobbed through the first 30 minutes of our session. When she learned that I had a headache, she gave me some Tylenol and Benadryl and within 30 minutes, I felt 100% better. Probably thinking, "this lady needs to relax, She even sent the Massage Therapist my way for a shoulder massage. she gave me some Ativan while we were waiting for my infusions to be mixed by the pharmacy. After the Ativan, my sobs were mixed with hysterical laughing at the compassion and humorous postings on my Facebook wall.

Eventually, I made it through and was home way earlier than I thought I would be (5:30—after we ate dinner at my favorite restaurant). I was happy that by the time I left, I was able to look Jillian in the eyes, smile and thank her profusely for all she had done.

So, it was not at all what I had anticipated (pain, burning in the veins, Constant feelings of nausea, shortness of breath, dizziness, etc.) Of course, I am trying not to anticipate side effects that may surface, although I am prepared to deal with them.

When i think about all the spontaneous sobbing, I'm confused. Maybe it is all the "processing," But, then maybe it was missing my friend who had passed on who walked beside me on this journey during my early morning meditation, you know, the one who had rescued me for 8 years.

6-16-17

ENERGY POINTS

I knew that I just had a certain amount of "energy points" available for the day, so I doled it out in my mind, hoping to accomplish three tasks. The first task was a "must" as I had an OT appointment to learn about lymphedema as a possible side effect of my future radiation and how to avoid it. The second task was to pick up my prosthesis at the specialty shop about five miles from the rehab building. The final task on my list was to go grocery shopping. This was important to me because my appetite is practically nonexistent and I wanted to walk around the store to see if anything "looked appetizing" to me.

Garry, the OT covered several concepts, showing me how to massage my 11-inch scar and how to keep my lymph fluids moving, not only on my right quadrant, but throughout my entire body.

"My 11 o'clock appointment canceled," he said, addressing his computer. "Do you have time for some extra instruction? I have a few more things I'd like to show you."

"We have all the time in the world," said my enthusiastic husband who had been diligently taking notes up to this point.

Hmmm. I thought—time, yes. Energy? I don't think so. I had been sitting in one position for an hour attentively following instructions and I could feel the clock ticking on my energy credits. Advocating for myself is something I am trying hard to learn, but it is difficult as I know if I allow Michael to push me a bit harder than I push myself, I will do better. But I sat up and said it, "We have all the time in the world," I agreed, "but I'm not sure how much more energy I have." Garry looked at me compassionately, listening to my concern.

"What if I just show you two more exercises and then we'll call it a day?"

I agreed that I could learn two more exercises and I did. Eventually, we were on our way to the specialty shop to pick up my new bra and prosthesis, which I figured would be a quick in/out and on our way.

The chime sounded as I entered the shop, which is like entering a wonderland of possibilities for the person who needs accommodations in clothing. The salesgirl and owner came out and said she would be right with me. I took a seat next to another lady who I assumed was next in line. Just walking into the store took a lot of my energy and I could feel my allotment dwindling quickly. And then there is always the bathroom issue when you are on chemo. Using the bathroom, I came back out and sat down for about 45 seconds before saying, "you know, I think I will just come back later." The lady next to me perkily replied, "Okay, but I know she is almost done."

"I know," I said, "but I'm exhausted. I'll come back."

I got in the car and told Michael what was going on. He pulled away. Less than a block away, I realized I had left my purse at the shop, so he turned back. He went in to get it for me and then came out, "They are ready for you now if you want to pick up your stuff." he said. So, once again I got out of the car and sat down in the shop. The saleslady, who is a gem of a lady, asked my name and then went to find my items. She sat next to me with an intimately caring air about her.

"How are you doing?" she asked. And the thing about certain people is that when they ask you that question, you feel like they can see inside your soul and you can't possibly dismiss them with a word like, "fine" which basically stands for *Feelings Inside Not Expressed.*

"I'm exhausted and can hardly function," I said, tears slipping down my cheeks.
"Honey, listen. It gets easier. Are you just starting out?"
"Yes, I'm just 5 days post first chemo and I'm just so tired of not having any energy."

"You can do this." she encouraged. "I'm a 22-year survivor. I was diagnosed with Stage 4 breast cancer and they gave me six months to live. I had 2 small children. You can do this."

And I know I can, but at the moment I can hardly put a thought together in my mind other than, "just give me my stuff and let me go home." Our talk attracted the attention of the other 'survivors' in the shop and pretty soon I was surrounded by much UNWANTED support and hugs. Being an introvert w/ a low white cell count, the LAST thing you want is to be hugged by a bunch of strangers.

Fifteen minutes later, the lady was carrying my bag to my car for me, continuing to try to minister to my weak spirit. "Do you like plants?" she asked. I looked at her, trying to keep at least a little bit of kindness in my voice.

"No, I don't." I said, "Actually, you know what? I DO like plants, but right now I am working so hard on just keeping myself moving and taking the next step that I am not allowing anything else to distract me."

She looked at me compassionately and I could almost see her mind traveling back to a moment when she was a young mother of two with six months to live, "I understand."

And you know what? I think she really did.
6-19-17

THE DOWN & DIRTY OF CHEMOTHERAPY

The most I remember them saying about how chemotherapy would be is, "everyone responds differently, but here is a list of at least 40 different side effects you might experience" emphasizing once again that everyone responds differently. I appreciate that emphasis because I learned very early on in my diagnosis not to compare my journey with the journey of others. A diagnosis may bring a treatment that is basically a "walk in the park" for one person and the same/similar diagnosis may bring a treatment that requires another person to crawl across a swinging bridge suspended over waters of fire while alligators are continuously snapping at his/her heels."

I did, however, ask people about their chemo experiences. I found it to be something people hesitant to describe because it involves a lot of "down & dirty" details. A common experience shared, however, was the "third day following chemo is the worst" theme. So, imagine my surprise when I woke up the third day after chemo with great concern.

"Michael," I shook Michael out of his sound sleep first thing in the morning.
"What?" his eyes fluttered open looking a bit alarmed.
"I think there is something wrong with me." I stated matter-of-factly.
"Why?"
"Because, honestly, I feel better today than I have felt in my 57 years of life. What is with that?"
"Thank the Lord," he said. Then, we proceeded to get up and go about our separate routines—him, eating his cereal before hitting the lake for early morning kayaking. Me, enjoying some yoga joint rotations, breakfast, and reading.

"I'll be back to take you to your physical therapy around 1:15" he reminded me before heading off to work.

"I'll be ready." I promised.

So it was while I was sitting in the therapy office with two therapists and Michael when the bone pain started. It was if someone had wrapped me in a blanket and then slammed sledgehammers into my body.

The day of chemotherapy had concluded with the nurse applying a patch to my belly. "This is your white cell boost. Instead of coming in for a shot, this will inject you in about 27 hours with a dose of Neulasta which will keep your white blood cell count steady following chemo."

Michael and I both were intrigued with the technology of this patch which flashed a green light every five seconds to let us know everything was a "go." That night, every time I got up to use the bathroom, I looked like a walking lighthouse with the green light flashing beneath my night shirt. And then, 27 hours after my chemo was complete, it injected the Neulasta through a cannula and was removed 45 minutes later. They had listed bone pain as the main side effect, so I was expecting some knee or elbow pain, but I was not prepared for the intense lower back pain I was experiencing at this moment during my therapy.

As we were walking out to the car, I told Michael I needed to go home. I sat through a quick lunch at Cracker Barrel and then home we went. I crawled into bed and tried to find relief in sleep. The next six days are a blur of pain, nausea, diarrhea, rinse the mouth to help with mouth sores, nausea, diarrhea, sleep, repeat. They had said my appetite might be affected, but I've never had problems eating EVER so I was surprised when I could eat NOTHING. I did manage to drink water consistently, but food was not going to be going into my mouth.

Michael diligently tried to feed me my favorites and managed to get me to eat a few popsicles and on one occasion, some meat. It was always a 3-4 bite meal and then I was done. At the end of the six days, I had lost 10 lbs. From Monday afternoon to Sunday morning, I felt like I had danced with death.

And then the Sabbath dawned. I had decided I needed to read the book on strategies for dealing with chemo again, made a list of some foods I thought I could eat and sent Michael to the store. He dropped the groceries off before heading off to work and before even putting them away, I made myself a tortilla with egg and cheese. It was the best tasting tortilla with egg and cheese that I had EVER had. I ate another one. An hour later, I ate some baked beans. And later, something else. I felt my strength and appetite coming back and now...four days after my dance with death ended...it seems like a distant memory...like a quickly forgotten childbirth.

I know it is a dance I have to do at least five more times, but I can do that. My heart goes out to people I know who are doing this dance far more than I have to and it is not a beautiful dance. It is a dance full of down and dirty, but people do it and they do it with their heads held high, trying to maintain some dignity while absorbing the blows of swinging sledgehammers.

FULL CRANIAL PROSTHESIS

Even though I spent 24 years of my career as a teacher, I am not always so interested in learning all about a subject —especially if the subject is me or focused on me, but I am surprised when I encounter a feeling that I am not familiar with or that does not match my perception of who I am. It happened to me yesterday.

I figured as long as my friend, Terry, was here with me for a few days, I would take the plunge and my prescription for a "full cranial prosthesis" and get a wig. I am comfortable with my bald head, but I know others may not be and I'm not necessarily comfortable with just anyone seeing it yet.

I thought it would be "fun"—kind of like shopping for a new dress or a pair of shoes, so when we walked into the first shop full of beauty supplies in downtown Kalamazoo, I was surprised at how uncomfortable I felt. We did a quick once over of what they had and then left.

"I'm so surprised at what I am feeling," I confessed to Terry in the car, trying to sort out for myself what exactly was going on inside. "I just did not see anyone in there that I felt would understand the walk I'm on. I can't believe that is so important to me and that I'm not more open."

"But, you don't know that for sure, they might totally understand."
"I know. I didn't really give anyone a chance." I admitted.
"That's okay," assured Terry, trust your gut and if you aren't comfortable, we can try someplace else."

We drove to another wig shop that afforded a bit more personal attention and privacy, waiting patiently for the one available clerk to help us.

While Terry and I waited, we talked about the wig possibilities—a long, blond curly one (Michael's preference) or a short dark brown one, more like a hairstyle I would wear. Finally, the clerk appeared.

"How can I help you?" she asked.

I showed her my prescription, "Can you just explain to me how this works? I assume my insurance will pay for this, so how do you handle this?" I ask, unsure of whether or not I even wanted to do this.

"You need to pay us, we give you a receipt and then the insurance reimburses you."

I felt out of my element as Michael tries to make my journey more tolerable by dealing with all of the insurance issues .

"Maybe I should call them and see how much they cover so I know what I can look at." I decided that was a good idea. So, while I did that, the salesclerk kindly questioned Terry about my former hairstyle and they talked together in the other room while I made the call.

I sat there quietly after discovering our insurance would not pay anything for a wig, trying to process how I felt about that. I was okay with that as I didn't really want anything else to mess with and I definitely did NOT want one of those styrofoam heads anywhere in my house to haunt my dreams. PLUS, what if a wig was hot? What if I looked ridiculous? Who would I be if I wore a wig? What if it made me sweat? What if, What if, what if. How would I define myself if I wore a wig? If I wore it once, would I have to wear it all the time? But then, relief swept over me...the insurance made the choice for me. I could go home now.

We headed home, somewhat discouraged. Terry asked if I wanted to stop at the Beauty School and pick out a free one. The resources sheet said the School offered a limited choice of free, used donated wigs. I just wanted to go home. I didn't want to wear the wig of someone whose family had to remember to drop it off in a donation box after the funeral.

After we got home, Terry spoke to my insurance as my advocate to make sure I had understood correctly that they would not pay for one at all. Once confirmed, she asked me if she could call the Beauty school and see what they had to offer. I agreed.

After talking to a representative at the school, she felt so confident that this could be a positive experience for me and with my permission, made an appointment for me to go the next day to look at their wigs, which were no longer donated. The policy had changed since the handout I received and they were actually prepared to fit me for a free brand new wig that they receive through the American Cancer Society.

Arriving at the appointment with my turban-covered bald head, I was a bit nervous about a "young person" fitting me with a wig. This was NOT a "fun" thing in my mind anymore. I didn't want a young girl trying to make me feel like I was "cool" looking or "rocking" anything. I preferred privacy, modesty, and honesty.

After filling out a quick form and conversation with the trainer/fitter about my hairstyle preferences, Terry and I were escorted to a private room by one trainer and two young hair stylists who were being trained on how to fit a wig.

They had pulled some short dark styles for me and one blond curly wig (for a selfie to show Michael). The young girls were busy with the wigs while I pulled off my turban and the trainer put a stocking base on my head. There were no stares, no discussion, no humiliation. As I tried on different wigs, the young girls made sensible comments and voiced their preferences. We all agreed on a wig similar to my own preferred style.

When I walked out the young man at the front was kind and complimentary, telling me it looked very natural.

As we walked out, tears poured down my cheeks at the kindness of people I had encountered that day, including my awesome friend, Terry— who pushed just a little for me to get something that she knew might make my life a bit better.

In this cancer journey, I find myself having to "redefine" parts of who I am over and over, but today was different— I really felt like I got back a little bit of my dignity and myself when I walked out of that school.
7-19-17

DELIGHTFUL DISTRACTIONS

Approximately 20 years ago, I was in a Dollar store in South Haven, MI with a friend of mine. Inspired by a story I had recently read about a couple hiding an item in their home throughout their marriage just for fun, I decided to start the same tradition in our home. I searched the store high and low for the ugliest item I could find. That was the day, "BF (Biker Frog)" joined our family. As I slapped down my dollar + tax on the counter, I quietly welcomed BF to the Tupper marriage.

I named the game the "forever game," between Michael and I. Since I did not foresee our relationship ever ending, I could not think of a better name. And IF our relationship did ever end, I was quite sure I would have no hesitation relinquishing custody of the item to Michael. Fortunately, BF is still a part of our family. He has traveled in briefcases, pillowcases, perched on top of lamps, pianos, sat next to coffee cups in cupboards, hidden in boots, shoes, sock drawers, couch cushions, on top of computers, office drawers, and after spending almost a month beside the garden tub that Michael uses several times a week, I found him this morning in my microwave. I always find a smile on my face when I find him because I know Michael was thinking intently about me when he was looking for the best place to hide him.

In my cancer journey, smiles are hard to come by. But, I usually am blessed with one day every three weeks that I am energized and feeling pretty normal (day 1 post chemo). On that day, I try to do a big project in the house with rest periods every few hours. Today, my project was cleaning cupboards and shelves in my kitchen.

Other days throughout the month, I will have minutes to hours of these "energy gems" where I will work on my 12-steps, read, or try new decor on my bald head. I can't even remember when working all day with only a lunch break was a possibility and I am ashamed that I did not appreciate those days more, but hopefully I will eventually have the opportunity to do that again some day.

So, for today anyway, I am so thankful for delightful distractions that raise the quality of my life on a journey where that is a constant concern. Today, I am so thankful for the ugliest thing I could find at a Dollar store 20 years ago and that on that day that Biker Frog joined our family, "forever" as a delightful distraction.

SIDE EFFECTS OR PSYCHO EFFECTS?

In the summer of 2008, I spent three months traveling around the midwest speaking at a number of churches representing Henderson Settlement in Frakes, KY as well as speaking about our own mission assignment at the Hope United Methodist Church.

During that time, our health insurance plan provided an "Ask-the-Nurse" service, encouraging us to call a toll free number to ask questions rather than going to the ER.

I sat in the parking lot of a mall in northern Indiana and dialed the number because I was experiencing some bleeding that I was concerned about, especially since I was taking a blood thinner.

"Ask-A Nurse. Please hold a nurse will be with you shortly."
I waited a bit for the nurse to arrive. "Can I help you?"
I explained the nature of my bleeding.
"Well, Lori, I can understand your concern. I would like to ask you some questions before I advise you, is that okay?"

"Sure," I said, ever the cooperative patient.
"Do you have a headache?" I touched my head and at that moment I realized there was a dull ache hovering somewhere in my head.
"Actually, I do have a bit of a headache," I admitted.
"Okay. Do you feel nauseous?" I put my hand on my stomach and was uncertain if I was feeling nausea or hunger. It WAS lunchtime.
"Um...yeah, I think I do feel a little bit of nausea."
"Okay. Are you lightheaded at all?" I looked around the enclosure of my car quickly, catching just a hint of lightheadedness.
"Yes. I am a little bit light headed."

"Okay. Are you sweating at all?" Seeing as it was the middle of summer and I was sitting in a car without air conditioning, this was a no-brainer.

"Yes. I am sweating."

"Well, Lori, based on my assessment, I think you need to go to the nearest ER." Suddenly, it hit me that I felt much better before I talked with the nurse. "Thank you. I will consider that" I said as I hung up, following up with my own assessment, "Based on mine, I think I just need to stop talking with you, get out of this hot car, and eat some lunch!" That was the day I stopped reading the side effects of drugs. Sometimes I will have Michael read them just so he is aware, but I find if I read them, I experience each one as my brain processes it—not a good thing. In fact, if someone is talking to me about their own health issues, I find myself experiencing the very same symptoms as they describe it! So, it was with great trepidation that I fingered the "bluebook" the chemo nurse had given me on May 30. I wanted to be an informed patient and I wanted to be aware of the side effects of the drugs being pumped into my body, BUT I wanted to avoid the psycho effects that sometimes grip my suggestible brain.

So, now I spend every day of my chemo cycle managing side effects. I know every body is different, but I am amazed anyone could ever work while they were having chemo. I find I have about an hour of energy and then require an equal amount of time to rest. And now that I'm halfway through the tough chemo, I know the routine— chemo, then 1 great steroid day, followed by a week of constant rest, pushing through the bone pain, trying to keep the nausea at bay, taking my temperature, fighting yeast and thrush infections, and doing as little as possible. The next week is what I call my "poop week" where I feel like all I do is crave food, but IF I choose to eat—I pay the price. After this week, I start to feel better, am hungry ALL THE TIME and everything begins to heal up, but I still require a lot of rest. And then...it is time for the next chemo. Halfway through, and this has become my new normal, but at least I know how to plan (lunch appts. and social things need to fall the week before chemo) and I know there is hope. I know how many more times I have to live through poop week and how many more great steroid days I can count on.

I share this, not to complain, but to inform you of how blessed I feel to at least know what to expect and how thankful I am I don't have to call Ask-a-nurse for every little (or big) side/psycho effect.

THE PRAYER I DIDN'T PRAY

The Cancer Center...my healing space. This is the place I was ask to go to one day every three weeks to trust people I didn't know to pump dangerous poisons into my body. It is a pleasant place...a snack cart, free massage, TV if you want, ice water around every corner, free crocheted caps...and puzzles. Who wouldn't trust a place with puzzles?

So when I heard he had been accepted to volunteer in MY healing space—I felt panic and fear. He was the bully from our last church...the man who tried to get my husband, a minister called by God, fired every week by sending emails to the "higher ups." He ambushed, disrespected, and tormented my family. He spread rumors, distrust, and unhappiness. Yet, at the church, I always put on my minister's wife mask and treated him with respect. I tried to treat him how I wanted him to treat my family, but now he was going to be volunteering in my healing space. What did that mean? How could I heal if he was present with his negative energy? I felt like I would be a hen walking into a henhouse guarded by the proverbial wolf. Should I transfer to a different center? Should I write and ask him to resign? I didn't know how to pray—only worry.

God, do you really expect me to learn even more ways to be nice to him? Really? Don't you think that is a bit much to ask of me when I'm already fighting cancer and going through chemo?

As we left the center following my third chemo, he was at the door. "Have a blessed day" he said. I kept my hands tensely to my side trying to keep any stray fingers from popping up. How could he use that "holy" language with me after he had tried to rip our lives apart? How could I heal if he was present?

Sleeplessness ensued for the next three weeks. What could I do? I thought about writing the CEO of the cancer center, I thought about changing infusion centers, I thought about stopping my chemo altogether. The only prayer I had the courage to pray was that God would help me sleep.

The night before my 4th chemo, we had dinner with some mutual friends (of the bully). I opened up to my friend and told her how anxious it made me to have to face the bully when I went to the cancer center...my healing space.

"You don't have to worry about it anymore," she assured me. "I'm quite sure he quit." I couldn't believe it. A very heavy burden rolled off my back in that split second. And it was true.

The next morning I got up early to go to my healing space. As I walked into the building of trusted strangers, I gave thanks to God for the answer to the prayer I did not have the courage to pray.

ANGELS EVERYWHERE

It was 2003. Sarah and I were heading back home to Pentwater from Indiana and she was anxious to get home and finish some homework for school the next day. I, on the other hand felt the need to stop for dinner. I was on a strict diet at the time and knew I needed to eat, preferably at Bob Evans where I could get a healthy salad.

Sarah was livid with me and threw a teen- age temper tantrum. I sat and slowly ate my salad while she glared at me with tears running down her cheeks, refusing to order anything to eat herself. As we sat there, we talked, but not much. After about 20 minutes an elderly lady walked up to Sarah, knelt to her level, threw her arm around Sarah's shoulder, looked into her eyes and said, "I just want you to know Jesus loves you." Then she got up, turned around and left the restaurant. Sarah and I both were so shocked, we sat there for about 20 seconds and then we both burst out laughing. It was all that was needed to break the tension between us. I ate a little faster as we talked for the remainder of the meal and then we were back on the road. *Angels Everywhere.*

Today, Michael and I went to a grocery store 40 minutes away to pick up a few items that were on sale. As we walked out to the car, I offered my cart to an African- American woman and she took it, thanking me quietly. I had just sat down in the car when she was at my window. "I know this might sound weird, but my name is 'Oran' and the minute you offered me your cart, I felt strongly that I need to say a prayer for you. Do you mind if I say a prayer for you right now? I gave her my hand and immediately thought, "how beautiful our hands look holding on to each other."

She asked my name and then proceeded to pray a beautiful prayer of healing for me. Tears of hope ran down my cheeks and I felt my fears subside. I did not have the composure to share my journey with her, but I thanked her sincerely as she squeezed my hand. I felt the love of God flowing through from her to me and I pray she felt it returned from me to her. As we drove away from her, I looked at Michael and said, "THAT must be why we drove so far to come to the store today."

Angels Everywhere!

PRACTICAL WAYS TO MAKE THE CANCER JOURNEY EASIER

1. Don't compare your journey to anyone else. It will not be as easy or as hard as others you talk to. Everyone's journey is unique so hang on for the ride!

2. Don't let yourself become a "cancer elitist" Just because someone has not had as much surgery, chemotherapy, radiation or other treatments doesn't mean they didn't walk the ridges of hell from the time they heard their cancer diagnosis till the time they had a plan. That emotional walk is what a cancer diagnosis is.

3. Set up comfortable environments for yourself that you do not mind being in. I found three that I favored: 1) my bed (with the option of Netflix on the TV); 2) My recliner (w/ my laptop close by, a stand for water. books, and a blanket.) I could also charge my laptop and my phone at the table; 3) The guest bedroom for alternative positioning if I was uncomfortable at night.

4. Don't be afraid to ask for anxiety medication, especially when you are first dealing with a diagnosis of cancer. Sometimes we need help resting and coming to terms with our mortality can be a bit anxiety-producing!

5. Pay attention to what you need to be comfortable. If the chemo makes you hot, have fans available in your spaces. If it makes you cold, shower your spaces with coverups, shawls, and quilts.

6. Purchase over-the-counter items you may need to address side effects BEFORE you start the chemo and put them in a container in another room in order to avoid the, "I'm uncomfortable at 3 am" run to a 24-hour pharmacy. Even if you never use the items, it will be a comfort to know they are available.

7. Block off the months you will be having chemo and don't plan anything. Stick with, "I will have to see how I feel" as a standard answer when asked to obligate yourself.

8. Eat when and what you feel like eating. Chemo can cause a lot of nausea, but not eating at all will make it worse. Stay on top of your nausea by taking the nausea medication consistently and by eating small portions. Don't be afraid of things like Boost. I found the protein concentration in a Boost made me feel better—especially first thing in the morning.

9. My chemo affected how things tasted, which is awful for someone who enjoys eating like I do. So, I had a candy bowl that I allowed myself to eat from whenever I felt like it. I filled it with strong tasting candies (junior mints, Good & Plenty, extreme sour patch kids, tootsie roll pops). I know sugar isn't the best thing for you to snack on, but sometimes I just needed something I could taste.

10. Put a toilet extender seat on your toilet for while you are on chemo. It will simply help you to save some energy during a time of extreme fatigue and every little bit helps.

11. Learn to change how you feel by changing your position. Sometimes, just sitting up instead of laying down will help a lot.

12. Do what you want to do. I watched a lot of Netflix until I could concentrate enough to read. I even played Candy Crush because there were times when I just needed my brain to concentrate on something besides cancer.

13. Use a lint brush roller when your hair starts to fall out. What they don't tell you is that it actually hurts when your hair starts to fall out and it is frustrating when your head looks "mangy." I actually brushed my scalp with a soft toothbrush, which helped with the "mangy" look and felt good on my scalp.

14. I had a horrible gag reflex right after each chemo for about 2 weeks, which meant I couldn't really brush my teeth as usual, so I would use just a

soft toothbrush with warm water to scrub them if I could and then baking soda as I could tolerate it.

15. If you are "crashing and burning," don't be afraid to put up a 'no visitors' sign if people stop by. It takes an enormous amount of energy to interact when you are on chemo and you want to save those energy credits to do the things that are important to you.

16. Drink lots of water or gatorade—stay hydrated. You will feel better if you do.

17. Document side effects and drugs you take especially at the beginning so you can become somewhat familiar with how your cycle will be and when you can expect to have to be near a bed for rest or a bathroom for other side effects.

18. Keep all the cards and notes you get to encourage you throughout your treatment. I hung an "encouragement clothesline" in my dining room (given to me by my daughter) and kept it up the whole time I was having chemo. I added extra special cards that spoke to me and pictures people gave me. I loved it!

19. Be honest about how you feel. If you don't feel good —don't feel badly about it, just state it and do what you need to do for yourself. It doesn't matter if anyone understands how badly you feel. Just do what you need to do for yourself.

20. If you want to cry—CRY. It is okay. It sucks to have cancer and it is okay to be sad about it.

21. If you don't want to be brave—don't be brave. Be who you are in the moment, but know that you might feel differently in an hour.

22. If you have a difficult time sleeping, listen to a guided meditation on YouTube, it will help you sleep and they have nice ones on healing as well...and they are free.

23. If you or someone around you can keep the area around you picked up and cleaned up, you will feel better. Clutter tends to make you feel crowded and you will probably feel the need for more space when you feel badly, not less space.

24. Don't worry about losing weight and exercise while on chemo. Do what you can activity wise, but don't beat yourself up if you can't do

something everyday. Fatigue is real and some days you might not even be able to move between bed and a chair very easily.

25. Talk to your body and tell it what you want and need. Pat yourself on the back for making it through each step. You will be surprised at how your body will honor many of your wishes and how good you will feel when you acknowledge how hard you are working to get well.

26. Countdown treatments and accomplished tasks. Getting chemo can be boring because you spend a lot of time just resting. As you countdown treatments, you at least feel like there is some progress in your life. I took a picture of myself beside the same tree every month to document my "look" and the seasons. After my treatment, I made a wooden photo board with the pictures in order and titled it, "A year in the life of a tree & me." It is a reminder of a difficult journey that I traveled.

QUALITY OF LIFE

Following our first wedding anniversary, at the ages of 20 and 19, Michael and I packed up our little apartment in eastern Illinois into a small U-Haul, hitched it up to our Pinto station wagon and then made the long trek to Kansas City, Missouri, where he would attend the Nazarene seminary and I would work as an editorial assistant at the Nazarene Headquarters. It was a pretty protected environment and my world was small at that point, hanging out with only people who believed the same as I did.

In an effort to "fit in" (I never felt like I did), I signed up for a "beauty class" with my co-workers. It was called "Images of Loveliness" and the goal was to mold us into "ladies"—kind of a charm school if you will. So, for the next 12 weeks we learned about posture, hair care, skin care, poise, nutrition, color analysis, fashion, appropriate conversation, wifely duties, spirituality, hygiene, nail care, entertaining etiquette, and a number of other lessons that I found quite challenging.

One of the biggest challenges in my life is that I have always just been me. As hard as I try to be someone else, the me in me just sneaks out and it seems that is all I can be. But, during those 12 weeks, I worked very hard at being a different me. I monitored my words before I spoke them aloud, I didn't cross my legs at the knees, I ate a lot of fish, and I certainly did not wear red. At the end of the day, my life was filled with, "I should have done that differently."

Our final class was a celebration and reward ceremony. Small trophies graced the podium where our leader very gracefully, with her perfect posture and proper conversation skills presented them. My friend, Carol, received the highest honor—"Miss Image of Loveliness." My friend, Pam, was presented the trophy for runner up Miss Image of Loveliness. Both ladies received trophies and gift cards to a local salon. There were other trophies presented for the most weight lost, positive attitudes, best dressed, etc. and then there was one left. Imagine my surprise when my name was called to receive the "overall most improved" trophy.

I am thankful that I was able to be gracious in the moment and was able to muster a poise-filled "thank you" while not wearing red. But then I went home and as I thought about my trophy, I doubted the honor of receiving it. Was I really THAT bad before the class? I kind of liked who I was before I learned you should drink warm water laced with lemon before you get out of bed...and sometimes I like to cross my legs at the knees, and I love red!

As I thought about my experience, I realized those 12 weeks were filled with negative, self-doubt, thoughts of who I SHOULD be and not thoughts of who God had made me. I determined then that "Quality of life" is determined by the words you say to yourself at the end of the day."

In the day-to-day, I have often been very hard on myself through the years...too fat, too tall, too much acne, hair not shiny enough, too lazy, too simple, too small-busted, too...too...too.

So, in February, 2017 when I heard the words "breast cancer" one of my first thoughts was, "Great! There goes my quality of life down the tubes." I immediately pictured myself laying in a rented hospital bed in the middle of a darkened living room, surrounded by medical equipment and quiet nurses while Michael sat thoughtfully in the corner, elbow on his knee and one finger across his mouth, deep in thought.

This image haunted me from the day I received the phone call until I woke up from the surgery removing my right breast, then it was gone.

Prior to my surgery, I had many conversations with my body explaining to it what was going to happen and that the cuts we were going to experience were cuts that would help us, not assault us. My body responded with making it through the surgery and healing quickly. My conversations with my body then changed to how my body was now different with only one breast. I kept waiting for the grief of losing a body part to fall on me, but found, for whatever reason, it never bothered me. There were only about five years of my life where I identified myself sexually by my breast and quite frankly, those years were mainly during high school.

After the insertion of my port, I felt more trauma than I had since my diagnosis. I felt like my body was trying to "spit it out" via infection and discomfort. So, we started talking again. I explained to my body how important the port was going to be when I started getting chemo. Amazingly, it understood and eventually accepted the port and allowed me to heal.

One of my biggest fears in having cancer and taking chemo was my quality of life. Would it change? Would it be so bad that I would spend my entire time in the bathroom? Would I be praying for death? Would I only be able to talk about cancer? Would I drive Michael away with my complaining? When I lost my hair, would I look like Uncle Fester from the Addams Family? What words would I be saying to myself at the end of the day?

But now I am on the other side of the experience and I find myself saying things to myself that I have never said to myself at the end of the day...

"Wow, Lori. I am so proud that you were able to handle that chemo experience without screaming."

"Yes, you cried, but that was okay. It is okay to cry."

"Thank you for being open to the people at church, that took a lot of courage."

The words I have been speaking to myself have been positive, affirming, and encouraging. It is almost like my quality of life has improved since my diagnosis as I am seeing a different person than I have ever seen.

People kept saying I was strong but I didn't believe them. I know my weaknesses and I know my fears.

Quality of life...my biggest fear when I received my cancer diagnosis, but IF... "Quality of life is determined by the words you say to yourself at the end of the day."

At the end of my days now, I say—I'm ok and I'm going to wear red.

RADIATION

In an effort to continue my documentation of my cancer journey, I want to share my radiation experience and what it entails.

My initial consultation with my radiology oncologist happened back in May when I met also with my chemo oncologist. The plan was to do chemo first (June-Sept.), have a few weeks off and then start radiation.

I finished my chemo on Sept. 29th and met with Dr. Radowski again on Oct. 4th. I was in the midst of my final crash and burn and I was so glad Michael was with me to comprehend the information he was trying to impress upon us. Seeing as I was on narcotics to help deal with the crash and burn side effects, I only remember wondering if he had gone to prom that spring and him trying to explain to me his reasoning in radiating my healthy lymph nodes. Yes, there would be a greater risk of lymphedema, but he felt the benefits outweighed the risks.

I decided in May that I was going to do the traditional treatment for my cancer and in deciding that, I also decided I was going to trust my team to make the right decisions for me. Less than a week later, I went in and they gave me 3 "tattoos" that would help line up the radiation treatment. I begged the girl to make them interesting (heart or boob-shaped), but she just apologized for her lack of artistic ability and just gave me the standard "freckle" ones—none of which I have been able to find on my body since!

A few days before my radiation was to start, Dr. Rad, who looks like he might have had his braces removed just last week before the Homecoming dance, called and left a message for me to call because he wanted to "change my plan." Ever the cooperative patient, I called right back and spoke with his nurse.

"Dr. Radowski wanted me to call because he wants to change my radiation plan," I explained. "Oh yes, I can explain that to you," the nurse said. "He wants to have you hold your breast while getting your treatment so your diaphragm will inflate and your liver will be pushed down out of the radiation field."

"Ok," I said, totally confused but wanting to be cooperative. "I assume I will hold my left one since I don't have one on my right side anymore." I reasoned.

"Pardon me?" She said sounding confused (to my great delight!)

"Well, I only have one breast," I reasoned, "so I assume you want me to hold my left one during treatment?"

She laughed. "Oh no, NOT your breast...we want you to hold your BREATH."

I was so glad she could not see my embarrassment. "Oh, ok—I can do that. I will practice before my treatment, but I'm pretty sure that won't be a problem."

Two weeks later, I started my treatments. The process is pretty simple. I check in with the receptionist and she gives me a pager. It is like the pager I might get at a restaurant like The Olive Garden, except when this one buzzes, it is time for ME to be the entree'. When it buzzes, I go to the dressing room, remove my clothing from the waist up, put on a hospital gown open in the back and another one over that open in the front (to cover everything hanging out). I put my own belongings in a locker and put the key around my wrist. Then I sit in the dressing room and talk to anyone else who might be there or watch the food channel until my pager buzzes again.

On the second buzz, I go to "my" machine. Mine is called the Spartan machine and my team greets me with—"Hi Lori, when is your birthday?" After telling them my birthday for three sessions, I start adding, "I would think you would know it by now!" They are sweet and always talk nice to me, asking what I've done with my day so far.

I always feel a little guilty at how little I have done with my day. I take off the gown open in the front, slip my right arm out of the one open in the back and lay on the sheet on the table. A bolster is placed under my knees and a large rubber band is placed around my shoes to hold my feet together. I fold my gown over so my right side is exposed and place my hands above my head (grabbing two bars) and turn my head to the left. Two technicians pull at the sheet I am laying on in order to straighten my body. I try not to help. After they say, "Perfect" (a word they use a lot in order to give me the illusion that at least one thing in my life is under control), they leave the room, closing the 8-inch thick door behind them.

Then it is just me and E.T. The bright red laser lights click on and I shut my eyes only because it seems like the smart thing to do. Machines move around me and I hear a voice say, "Okay Lori, when you are ready take a deep breath and hold it." I do, holding it from 8-20 seconds (depending on which zap they are doing). They do 6-8 zaps each treatment session, which involves about 15 minutes on the table. Every 5 sessions, they take extra pictures which turns my time into a 30-minute session.

When I am in my treatment, I look at E.T. staring at me and I wink at him and try to stare him down. He doesn't flinch as he continues to move certain panels around and do his job. I would actually talk with him, but I know the team can hear everything I say and I don't want them to think I am totally crazy.

When I am finished, they come in and help me off the table, ask my plans for the evening and then tell me they will see me the next day. I tell them "Thank you" and then change my clothes and head back home. If it is Friday, I meet with Dr. Rad and his nurse. They look at my skin and tell me it is going to get worse, but that it will eventually heal.

I try to be a pleasant person when I go fo my radiation. It is not fun, but my team is nice. I baked them chocolate chip cookies on the day of my 7th treatment to remind them it is more fun to bake cookies than people.

I trust them to do the right plan for me and I appreciate their positive interest in me and willingness to laugh at my silly comments. And even though I sometimes think they overuse the word "perfect." It is nice to pretend everyday from 3-3:15 that at least one thing in my life is under control.

JOURNEYS

Sometimes our journeys in life have to be traveled alone.

Michael and I both sat quietly, stunned by the words of the social worker we had been meeting with for over a year in our attempt to adopt a baby from South Korea.

"I'm sorry Mike and Lori," Marcia said, "I just cannot recommend you because I don't feel like Mike is nurturing enough to be a good parent and Lori, I don't think you can counteract that."

I watched her spewing the words, but could not comprehend why she was saying the words that were rolling off of her tongue. We had been working with her for over a year and this was to be our final session before recommendation for adoption after three miscarriages and seven years of trying to have children on our own.

We left her office incredibly sad and confused. She offered a gram of hope by agreeing that if we were cleared by a marriage counselor of her choice, she would recommend us. We agreed, feeling strongly bonded already to our emotional baby from Korea. We walked to the car, hand in hand, feeling remarkably empty—as if another miscarriage had just taken place.

Long story, short...the counselor recommended us highly and we ended up with the best son ever and a surprise pregnancy in the process, blessing us with the best daughter ever (four months apart to the day). But it was a quiet, lonely journey. The last thing we wanted to tell our friends is that the social worker thought we would be bad parents...so we held each other and plugged along, hoping our dreams weren't going to be buried unrealized...and that is what you do when you are on lonely journeys. You hold each other, you cry, and you try to find hope wherever you can—a flower, a child's innocence, an older person's wisdom, the sunshine.

And now, I wish Marcia could know Michael today. My husband who continued to make sure my "travel dreams" came true even after I was diagnosed with cancer in February. The man who carried my pink "goodie bag" out of the Women's Breast center because I didn't want to be associated with it. He who read the Breast Cancer Treatment book cover-cover when I refused to open it. The one who has kept track of every appointment and refuses to let me see bills and Explanation of Benefits from the Health insurance Company. I wish Marcia could see my Michael who has been at every single appointment (with the exception of one), every chemo treatment and every radiation treatment.

I think of Marcia often—especially when I get out of the car and Michael offers me his arm or holds my hand. I think of Marcia when, in the middle of the night, Michael slips his hand into mine or reaches over to rub my bald head. I think of Marcia when I watch Michael interacting with our two children, now 31 years old. Our two children who grew up with one of the most nurturing dads on this earth and who have a dad today who would travel any journey beside them no matter how lonely or incredibly sad it might be.

JOURNEY FOR THE WEAK

It is a journey for the weak
who are willing to listen to others say you are strong
You know better
as you run for the Zofran
and the Imodium
and the Senokot.
A journey that begins again each time the port is accessed with a deep
breath
and the poisons flow freely wrecking havoc on the bad and the good.
A trip you have purchased tickets to perhaps every time a farmer has
sprayed a field,
every time a diet drink is sipped, maybe even with the simple act of deep
breathing.
As you travel the path,
there are many companions and yet, you are hauntingly alone.
Nobody really wants to see your pictures
from this journey.
No poses in front of the healing center with
smiles and rabbit ears sticking up from your bald head. No fashion
shows praising your creative sense with coverings, trying to hide from
others that you feel like crap while shopping for produce.
Day after day includes various side trips to the land of side effects
Demanding questions,
Denying the fears
Dwelling in the lands of possibilities and Dwindling
expectations
Defying Discouragement
Oh, you believe you might make it, but,
it will be like arriving at your destination
only to find your luggage was left behind
back at the station where you were willing to listen to others say
you are strong and you knew better.
8-9-17

AFTER THE JOURNEY...

Less than a year following my treatment, I took a writing class for cancer survivors. Here are some writings that materialized from that class...

CHANGES

It begins with blame...whose fault is it? What is the reason? The why questions are what eats at me most. Did I do something wrong? I always followed the exam rules, but the rules must have changed. Change sucks and makes me tender. Before the baldness there were so many more places to hide, but now I am exposed, so raw, so naked. Was it better before? I don't know--Maybe, maybe not.

Change sucks, and yet ...maybe I get to be a new me and that is okay. I feel more deeply, love more easily. I am slower and more tender. I am more tolerant and giving. I am a new person--a better person--a person with hope and less fear. A person with no fear of death and more importantly, no more fear of living. How often I say now, "I can do this! I've had cancer. I've faced death, what do I have to lose? I've pumped my body full of poisons and have survived so far and even though they may not guarantee my survival, I can guarantee each moment will be better, sweeter, kinder, and the fault will not lie in me or anyone else.

Hopefully, it will be THE big tragedy in my life that I am able to look back on and realize the loneliest journey was a journey I traveled with so many who love me and even though only I could walk the path spread before me, it was an important path for me to walk...a path with new rules, new directions, all leading to a new me--exposed, raw, and naked...changed, but better.

LOVER OF MY LIFE

On the path, I walk. Sometimes I long for you to be beside me--sometimes I long to be lonely. You have been so supportive, willing to organize my drugs, hold my puke basin, even offering to take my chemo for me--if only they would let you!

I wonder how this journey has affected you. Did you fear the outcome as much as I did? You always seemed to have such strength even while regretting the interruption in our retirement travels.

You always spoke survivor belief, calling me "beautiful," even though I would dispute and doubt. I often called you the "king of Denial" because I didn't think you were facing the reality that there are no guarantees or "cancer frees" for me.

And yet, I found your positivity wearing off on me. I found myself believing your encouraging words and pretty soon I found myself believing that I would survive.

Occasionally, I still question--how long before it returns? Will I fight again? And in my heart, I hope the answers will be there when I need them. I hope that when I am faced with my own mortality, I will embrace life as it is, feel the peace of your deep love, let you take me in your arms and together walk the path before us.

PERFECTION

Perfection, my old friend, is no longer here. Perfect is gone. Not sure when it left me. It was still a part of me as I learned handwriting. Painstakingly forming the letters of my name as a five year old. I felt its presence in later years as I practiced my name in cursive, including my last name as the one of my most recent "crush."

Perfection was still present with me as I morphed into adolescence--starting each day with a 2-mile run. And my friend followed me into relationships with boyfriends and eventually my husband, Michael.

And if things were not perfect, I would leave. Running away from the imperfect me and my imperfect world.

And then, at age 27, following a major stroke, NOTHING in my life was perfect any longer...not my relationships, not my life, and definitely NOT me!! Unable to read or compute numbers, I spent my time struggling through Dr. Seuss books and bouncing checks. Raising my two babies who were 4 months apart became such a challenge, trying to reason through new rules--no crossing the street by myself, no laughing in church, no walks without another adult. I was so limited in my efforts and so frustrated by my limitations. And then, I realized that life was a lot more comfortable when I embraced my imperfections.

My "quirkiness" was funny and fun! It was entertaining to realize my coat was on inside out and that it had been that way all morning. My friends would look at me with pity, but true happiness bubbled up inside of me as I gave up my perfect offerings.

Selling all the living room furniture when Michael was at a conference for a couple of days riddled him with frustration, but I found my self totally satisfied with the adventure.

Eventually, my brain healed from the stroke and I ALMOST fell into that perfection rut again, but then came the cancer diagnosis and the surgery that made me lose my perfection balance again. And it has been a year of giving up perfection again.

I look at myself in the mirror and I see the permanent radiation stain, the scar that replaces my right breast, the unruly curly hair that has replaced my bone straight pre-chemo hair, and I stare at that person and who I have become. She can still painstakingly form the letters of her name, but she is a totally different person from that five year old--a real bait and switch from whom her husband married 40 years ago. But, as she looks in the mirror today, she still feels... perfect.

CRACKED, BUT NOT BROKEN

When I was young, I used to believe stars were cracks in God's floor that allowed the light to shine through to us on earth. Cracks--so many cracks in life, often happening when things don't go according to OUR plan. Having a family (preferably 15 kids) turned into 7 years of infertility, an awesome son adopted from Korea and a daughter who makes her appearance exactly four months after our son is born. So much light flowing through the cracks of our years of frustration.

So many cracks in life--cracks in emotional stability and plans. I remember a short trip with my daughter, Sarah, to see family and her anxiety to get home to finish up some homework. At my insistence, we stopped for supper. As she engaged in a 16-year old temper tantrum because she did NOT want to stop, we put our relationship on the line. It was so close to not only cracking, but totally breaking apart.

I ordered a salad while she refused to order at all. Instead she sat across from me, tears streaming down her sweet cheeks as she tried to hurt me with her stares. I almost gave in. I almost thought I wasn't worth the time to stop, but I knew I was. I was not going to crack!

As we sat there in silence, I tried to enjoy my Cobb salad--the bacon being my favorite part! Sarah continued to ignore my appreciative comments and my offers to buy her dinner. I missed her voice--her constant chatter. We had always been fairly close and I longed to repair the crack in our relationship.

All of a sudden, an elderly lady walked over to Sarah, stooped to her level, put her arm around her shoulders, looked into her eyes and stated calmly, "I just want you to know, Jesus loves you!" and then she calmly stood up and walked out the door.

Sarah and I sat for about 20 seconds in silence, trying to process what had just happened. Did the lady think I had just given Sarah some horrible news? Did she think Sarah had just revealed some terrible secret to me?

Our eyes met. Suddenly we both burst out into hysterical, uncontrollable laughter, experiencing pure joy at the spontaneity and timeliness of a beautiful elderly woman.

I finished my salad while Sarah talked excitedly until I was done.
Such relief, such joy to be almost broken, but only cracked and then flooded with beautiful light!!!!

GUESTS

I lay in my bed after my port had been inserted. I literally was talking my body into accepting it. "It will make the chemo we have to take much easier--believe me you will be glad it is there when the time comes" I could feel the pushback and rebellion from my body. It felt as though it was actually trying to push it back out of its surgical opening, rejecting it as if it were a rancid watermelon. We talked often, my body and I.

The very first conversation I had with my body was about the surgery itself. Convincing my body that the interaction with a scalpel was NOT an assault, but a cut of salvation, preparing it for the trauma to come.

We talked often, my body and I. At one point, I even considered welcoming the cancer as a guest, but decided I did not want it to feel at home enough to stick around. My body and I became such great friends during that fighting year. I had made a sacred promise to it, committing myself to listen to every message it was sending me. And it, in returned, promised to do its best to heal.

As we both embraced the experience, I could see and feel clearly the decline during chemotherapy. My bloated, nauseous frame counted on good decisions regarding food I couldn't taste, but also allowed me the items that actually tickled my tastebuds like black licorice, junior mints, and sour patch candies.

We embraced our diagnosis and I felt my body finally allowing my port to become a part of us. And then, the radiation. Day after day of holding my breath as they tried one more method of attacking the cancer. And in this experience, new guest arrived at my heart house--a team of people who really seemed to care for me. We laughed and talked, and took care of business everyday for six weeks.

I was embarrassed after I was finished with all of my treatments, rang the bell, accepted the certificate, and then cried all the way to the car.

My husband, my support, asked compassionately, "Why are you crying?"

"It is so sad," I said "when the people you enjoy seeing the most are the ones shooting your body full of radiation that might kill you, but I will really miss seeing them every day!"

He wrapped his arms around me, "Let's go get a donut." And we did.

And then the burns began and the raw, purplish skin which is now a permanent stain.

The treatment/infusions continue--the new guests stream into my life in the form of side effects, ambushed emotions, and fatigue. And then it is over, the house is empty except for that first guest--my port--which will be leaving soon.

And I lay in my bed talking to my body and preparing it to heal without the port which will soon be gone.

Embracing it all moves me forward in my healing. Observing, commenting, and finding humor in it all kept me sane.

...baking cookies for my radiation team just to remind them, 'it is more fun to bake cookies than people.' We laugh.

...telling them that people would enjoy radiation more if the machine looked more like a tanning bed than an easy bake oven. We laugh.

...Comparing my bald head to Uncle Fester from the Addams Family. We laugh.

...Calling myself the great "uniboober" as opposed to a unibomber. And I laugh.

...Sharing my fantasy of burying my removed breast and marking it with a stone engraved with the word "busted." And I laugh.

I laugh, but so close to that laughter is a heart broken for the loss--and there are SO MANY losses—

...I will never be who I was before--the innocent, naive, safe-feeling girl who believed if I followed the monthly and yearly exams, I would be okay.

And yet even as I think of that, the laughter bubbles beneath the surface because I am so tickled pink to be who I am and I am so damn happy to be alive!!!

"NON-CONFORMIST"

Yes, I feel like a freak sometimes
and I know I am no longer the beauty queen.
Of course, this is much easier for me
because I never was.

I never cared so much how I looked.
I was the high schooler wearing her grandpa's shirts and
blue jeans with patches...a hippie born too late--flowers in the braided
hair.

Never a conformist, but conforming to who I thought I was.
And here I am now, pushing the 2nd half of life and loving the trauma
and adventure of it all

"ANDY ADDICTION"

"Serenely let us move to distant places and let no sentiments of home detain us."

I must have been around 13 years old when my mother explained to me that she never pictured us tied to an apron string. She preferred to picture her children attached to a very large rubber band that would stretch to allow us to go as far from home as we needed to, but having the flexibility to pull us back home if that was what we needed. I have always loved that image even though I have always preferred "home" to any other place on earth.

Even as a child, when my grandmother would give me the birthday gift of a week at church camp, there was always the temptation to refuse the gift as I would rather be home, listening to stories on LP records, rewriting them in play form and fantasizing which of the neighborhood kids could play each part. I was always the director and the star. But then, the reality was I would accept the gift of a week at camp where I was never the director or a star and I would often spend my free time on the phone crying for my mom to let me come home.

As I went through my year of cancer fighting, I often longed for those days of simplicity of just listening to stories. And that, well, THAT, my friend was how I developed my addiction to the Andy Griffith Show.

I needed something easy to understand and something with a happy ending, because I was so insecure in how my own ending was going to be.

And so, I started with the very first episode when Opie was so small and I watched the 8 seasons over and over--enjoying Barney's antics and Andy's determination to always make Barney the hero in spite of his crazy ideas and foibles. I always felt like Michael was my "Andy" as I was going through treatment. He always had my back and always let me shine no matter what.

As I would put on my daily Andy Griffith episode, I would feel my body physically relax as I entered a world where I knew no one was going to die or be badly hurt. It was so nice to visit Mayberry everyday, leaving behind the many pill bottles, head-covering choices, and fatigue. It was so nice to escape to a world that was simple, loving, and honoring.

Escape it was...at a time when I felt trapped by diagnoses, prognoses, medical terminology, and my own fears—

"Escape" was my manna--my 30 minutes of daily happiness and peace.

DREAMS

The experience gets farther and farther from me each day. It almost feels as if it were just a bad dream and that maybe it didn't even happen.

As I begin to rebuild stamina, re-integrate activities, and re-grow my hair, I feel ready for the next journey--whatever it may be.

This is the week my "encouragement line" will come down--the clothesline my kids hung in the dining room with flags of encouragement about my breast cancer--my favorite flag saying, "Cancer is shitty, sorry about your titty." How important that clothesline became to me throughout the year.

It presented itself initially when I arrived home from the hospital following my mastectomy. One of the flags said, "Secretly hoping chemo will give you Superpowers." It didn't, but I, myself, was secretly hoping it would as well.

The line grew with added attachments--birthday card, painted pictures given as gifts, get well cards, and love letters from friends. I promised myself the line would stay up until I was finished with my breast cancer journey.

And now, as I wait for the removal of my port, I feel my journey is close to over.

So, when my kids come home this week from the east coast, we will work together to restore my dining room back to its boring "before" status. But, my plan is to keep each flag and card just in case we need to resurrect the "encouragement line" for any reason in the future.

With the dismantling of the encouragement line, I think other things will be dismantled--maybe a good cleaning of the medicine chest--purging it of any narcotics and anti-nausea medications. It is such a relief not to have to live minute to minute. How tiring that became--to constantly be tuned to what my body was feeling and deciding which drug could restore normalcy. Always striving for that "normal" feeling, but not being able to remember exactly what "normal" was anymore.

The exhaustion colored the world so differently. A world that used to be so simple to understand presented complications that were difficult to discern. The fatigue made every action an effort and then embarrassment would reside where confidence used to live.

And even though support abounded, it was me who pulled back when others offered help. Pulling back, hoping I would soon wake up from this bad dream and find myself back in Mayberry.

"HAPPIEST GIRL"

"Say yes to everything, even if your fate sucks."

I woke up singing, "I'm the happiest girl in the whole USA" and then I walked into the bathroom, confused about the euphoric feelings sitting happily on my heart, swinging its legs back and forth to the rhythm of the refrain,

"Skippidy do da
Thank you oh Lord for making him for me
And thank you for letting life turn out the way
That I always thought it could be..."

Really? my life is all I always thought it could be? I couldn't wrap my mind around that concept as I planned out my medications for the day and chose the covering for my bald head. Finally, I said aloud, "Don't question it, Lori--just embrace the happiness .you are feeling...and I did. But, there is always this negative nagging trying to convince me that maybe I shouldn't be so happy. Maybe I'm delusional and in denial. So I look around and try to figure it out "logically."

...I did have a great time teaching school for 24 years.
...I have a family that adores me and will do anything to help me.
...I married the love of my life and we had mostly good years and we made it through the times that weren't so good!
...I have enjoyed a lot of different foods and music.
...I have a few friends that really understand who I am and love me anyway.
...I have walked the ridges of hell and soared the heights of heaven.

...I have suffered major illness that has brought huge changes not only to my life, but also to who I am at my core.

...I was happy and even though I was in the throes of chemotherapy, baldness, and medical tests, what was wrong with waking up to the song, "I'm the happiest girl in the whole USA?"

I have so many reasons to be happy...and that is okay.
"Shine on me sunshine
Walk with me world
It's a skippidy do da day
I'm the happiest girl, in the whole U.S.A."

LOVE OF FATE

"A mor fati,"--Latin for love of fate. Such an efficient way to live.

Love your fate. I wonder if Frank Gilbreath, the efficiency expert approached efficiency from that emotional standpoint?

I have often grown weary of people who overthink every situation--it takes so much time!!

At one point in my life, after my stroke, a beautiful lady from our church approached me,

"Lori, I know you have had a rough time lately and I just want to help you by offering to pay for anything you would like to do...you decide what you would like to do and I will pay for it.

~love of fate.

Such a gift. I told her I would think about it and get back with her soon. It was definitely something I "overthought."

Having just suffered a major stroke, I was so limited in everything I could do! Weak on my left side, I even struggled to pick up my two babies and I needed almost constant supervision myself because my reasoning skills were impaired as well as my physical status.

~love of fate

I suppose Juanita thought with me being new, overwhelmed mother, I might ask for a manicure, pedicure, or a day of free childcare. She probably didn't consider my weak reasoning skills. I pondered her offer for a week or so, trying to create something out of this gift. Finally, I knew what I wanted.

"Ok Juanita," I said the next time I saw her, "I know what I want." Her face opened up to me.

"I want to learn to play the saxophone." I announced. To her credit, she did not laugh, respond with words reminding me of my weak side, the glitches in my brain, or offer me a Kleenex to wipe the drool off the left side of my chin. No, she replied kindly, "okay, we will rent you a saxophone and I will pay for lessons for as long as you want to take them.

~love of fate.

The first day of lessons found me walking into a music store, the rented saxophone already hanging around my neck and excited to meet the new teacher who would make me a great musician.

He was probably only 3 years younger than me and I'm not sure what he thought of this 27-year old with a weak left side who often slurred her words.

~love of fate.

After about three weeks of lessons, he asked me, "Lori, what is your goal in learning to play the sax?" I didn't hesitate, "I want to play jazz."

Thankfully, he didn't laugh or roll his eyes, but walked to a bookcase in the back of the store and returned with a music book about one and a half inches thick with the word JAZZ splashed across its cover. He presented it to me and for the next four months I proudly practiced the songs in that book--adding a a simple jazzy "flair" to Row Row Row your boat, Happy Birthday, and A Bicycle Built for Two.

~love of fate.

THE GREEN SUCKER

I was about 4 years old and stood quietly on the stoop of my grandmother's small building that was the office for her medical practice. She had just given me my "BIG" vaccination and I had not cried because I wanted to prove I was a big girl and ready for school. But now, I stood quietly on the stoop with the rounded stick of the green sucker in my right hand, pulling the sucker in and out of my mouth.

Hot, salty tears slipped down my cheeks. The shot had hurt and it had been difficult to hold back the tears. Now that I was alone and no one I loved was watching me, I wanted desperately to curl up in a fetal position and just cry. I didn't want to discuss it or even tell anyone why—I just wanted to do it. But I didn't. After a few tears slipped out, I distracted myself with other activities and moved on.

I felt the same way this morning following my first mammogram since my breast cancer battle. I sat in the office remembering so many things from two years ago…the suspicion, the repeat mammogram, the biopsies, the "talk," the "goody bag," the ultrasounds, the rechecks, the drains, the pains, the bad coffee, the pamphlets, the referrals…and as I sat there waiting for the technician to return with the results of the films she had just squeezed out of my left breast, hot, salty tears slipped down my cheeks. I wanted desperately to curl up in a fetal position and just cry. I didn't want to discuss it or even tell anyone why—i just wanted to do it. But I didn't. After a few tears slipped out, I distracted myself with other thoughts and moved on.

The technician announced happily that the doctor felt everything looked "stable" and I didn't need to return until next year. I was relieved, but found myself wishing for a green sucker with a rounded stick.
1-23-19

MOVING ON

I wish I could say once the treatment is over—all is well. But, there are continuing side effects and trying to figure out which drugs are going to work.

I'm not sure the "new normal" will ever seem normal, but most days I am definitely happy to be alive.

I hope traveling this journey with me has been helpful to you in some way. Every journey is unique, so 1 in 8 women could probably self-publish their own journey and each story would be different. I'm thankful for my journey and the new me I have gotten to know. This is a poem I wrote very early in my journey to explain how I felt I was handling everything spiritually…

Lord,
Sometimes I think you are unreasonable in what you expect me to be able to handle.
You think I'm strong,
but I know I am very weak.
You think I'm flexible,
but I know how much I hate change.
You think I can help others,
but I know how much I think only of myself.
But, I know with you and the people you have sent into my life…everything will be okay.
Sometimes, I feel like you believe in me too much—
but more often I know I don't believe in you enough!
3-27-17

I wish you good health, a happy life, and mostly hope & peace as you walk the ridges of life.

ABOUT THE AUTHOR

Lori Tupper is a retired teacher and lives in Southwest Michigan with her husband, Michael. She has two grown children and enjoys being alive every second of every minute, every minute of every hour, every hour of every day, and every day of her life.